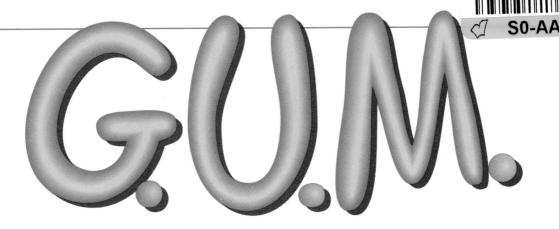

G.U.M.

Instruction and Practice for
Grammar, Usage, and Mechanics

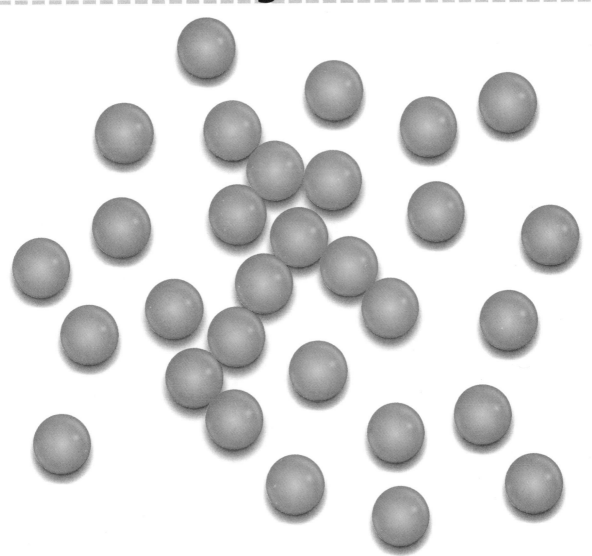

Zaner-Bloser, Inc.
Columbus, Ohio

Grade Level Consultants

Imogene Dantzler
Flint, Michigan

Barb Gavin
St. Louis, Missouri

Sue Pfersch
Brookfield, Wisconsin

Beth Smart
Inman, South Carolina

Gail Taylor
Inman, South Carolina

Developed by Straight Line Editorial Development, Inc., and Zaner-Bloser, Inc.

Cover photo: Rycus Associates Photography

Illustration: Tom Kennedy and Steve Botts

ISBN: 0-88085-810-9

Zaner-Bloser, Inc., P.O. Box 16764, Columbus, Ohio 43216-6764 (1-800-421-3018)

Printed in the United States of America

Table of Contents

Unit 1 Sentence Structure

Grab Bag **Hollywood**

Unit 2 Parts of Speech

The World Outside **The Sky and Beyond**

Unit 3 Usage

Beasts & Critters Insects and Spiders

Unit 4 Grammar

Unforgettable Folks Heroes

Unit 5 Mechanics

Looking Back **Ancient Civilizations**

Extra Practice

Unit Tests

Language Handbook

G.U.M. Indexes

Read and Discover

_____ Sound and movies came together in the late 1920s.
_____ Audiences could see and hear the action.
Write *S* next to the sentence with two or more simple subjects.
Write *P* next to the sentence with two or more simple predicates.

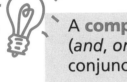

A **compound subject** is two or more subjects joined by a conjunction (*and*, *or*). A **compound predicate** is two or more verbs joined by a conjunction.

See Handbook Sections 10 and 11

Part 1

Each sentence has either a compound subject or a compound predicate. Circle the nouns that make up each compound subject. Underline the verbs that make up each compound predicate.

1. Engineers and technicians developed synchronized sound in about 1927.

2. Some silent movie actors looked attractive but spoke badly.

3. These actors left the movies and found other work.

4. Other actors adapted well to sound and had successful careers.

5. The great Greta Garbo spoke and laughed on film for the first time.

6. Her director and her fans were thrilled.

7. Critics and historians call the 1930s the beginning of Hollywood's golden age.

8. Comedies and musicals were popular in this era.

9. Musicals cheered and comforted audiences during the Depression of the 1930s.

10. Dancers coordinated their movements and performed complex routines in these musicals.

11. Circles and diamonds were popular dance patterns.

12. Hollywood actors, directors, and producers helped with the war effort during World War II.

13. They made movies about the war and entertained American troops abroad.

Fred Astaire and Ginger Rogers were a famous dance team in Hollywood.

Grab Bag

Part 2

Combine each set of sentences to form one sentence that has either a compound subject or a compound predicate.

14. In the 1950s, people regularly watched television. People went to movies less frequently.

_____

_____

15. Special film created a 3-D effect. Plastic glasses helped create a 3-D effect, too.

_____

_____

16. Monsters seemed to pop out of the screen. So did aliens. So did explosions.

_____

_____

Part 3

Write the answer to each riddle on the lines. Each answer is a compound subject or predicate from this lesson.

17. Who perfected the technology for movie sound?

__ __ __ __ __ __ __ __ __ and __ __ __ __ __ __ __ __ __ __ __
11 6 4 2 15   12   9   10   14   7 13 3 1

18. What dance patterns livened up 1930s movie musicals?

__ __ __ __ __ __ __ and __ __ __ __ __ __ __
                    5   8

Now use the numbered letters to answer this question:

What 1952 movie musical is about the transition from silent movies to "talkies"?

__ __ __ __ __ __ , __ __ __ __ __ __ __ __
1 2 3 4 5 6   7 8   9 10 11   12 13 14 15

Name _____

Grab Bag

Read and Discover

The stunt artist prepared her parachute in the plane.

Where did the stunt artist prepare her parachute? _____

> A **prepositional phrase** can tell *how, what kind, when, how much,* or *where.* A prepositional phrase begins with a **preposition,** such as *in, over, of, to,* or *by.* It ends with a noun or pronoun that is the **object of the preposition.** The words between the preposition and its object are part of the prepositional phrase. A prepositional phrase can appear at the beginning, middle, or end of a sentence.

See Handbook Section 19

Part 1

Underline each prepositional phrase. Circle the preposition that begins each phrase. Draw a box around the object of the preposition. There may be more than one prepositional phrase in each sentence.

1. An action movie is not an action movie without daring stunts.

2. Stunts are dangerous for untrained individuals.

3. Stunt artists often perform stunts for actors.

4. The director chooses a stunt artist with a similar physique.

5. The stunt artist dresses in the actor's costume.

6. With the right camera work, the audience will not notice the substitution.

7. A stunt artist might jump from a plane or onto a moving train.

8. He or she might cling to a cliff or run through fire.

9. Stunt artists train vigorously for their jobs.

10. They always take precautions for safety.

11. Stunts must look perilous, but they must not cause harm to anyone.

12. During a dangerous-looking jump, there is usually a net nearby.

13. Stunt artists tell their fans, "Don't try this at home."

14. Look for stunt artists the next time you are at the movies.

Grab Bag

Part 2

Rewrite each sentence below. Add at least one prepositional phrase to make the sentence give more information. Use phrases from the word bank or think of your own.

from a plane to the top	with expert timing over a car	in a pool of water in an instant	with a parachute on some mud

15. The stunt artist leaped. _____

_____

16. He landed. _____

_____

17. His foot slipped. _____

_____

18. He grabbed a rope. _____

_____

Part 3

Use the clues to complete the puzzle. Each answer is a preposition.

Across
2. The stunt artist strapped a parachute ___ her back.
4. The plane flew ___ a lake.
6. It circled ___ the spot where she would jump.
7. ___ a blond wig on her head, she looked a lot like the movie's star.
8. The stunt artist jumped ___ the plane.

Down
1. The wind whistled ___ her ears.
3. She flew ___ the air.
5. Then her parachute opened, and she floated ___ its great canopy.
6. ___ her safe landing, she gave the director a thumbs-up signal.

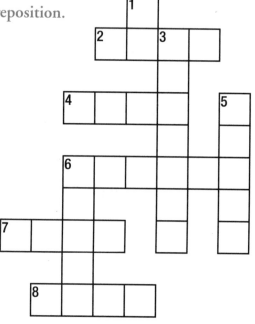

Name _____

Grab Bag

Read and Discover

Cinematic magic is created by a crew of talented technicians. ____
Many people work on different aspects of a movie. ____
Circle the simple subject in each sentence. Write *X* by the sentence in which the subject does something. Write *O* by the sentence in which the subject has something done to it.

If the subject performs an action, the verb is said to be in **active voice**. If the subject is acted upon by something else, the verb is said to be in **passive voice**. Many sentences in passive voice have a phrase beginning with the word *by*. Try to write most of your sentences in active voice.

See Handbook Section 17

Part 1

Write *A* if the verb in the sentence is in active voice.
Write *P* if the verb in the sentence is in passive voice.

1. First, a producer chooses a film idea. ____

2. The screenplay is written by a screenwriter. ____

3. The screenplay contains the movie's dialogue. ____

4. The screenplay also provides a guide for the filming process. ____

5. The screenplay may be changed by the director later. ____

6. The shooting schedule is developed by the production manager. ____

7. The casting director chooses the movie's actors. ____

8. Actors usually read lines from the screenplay for their auditions. ____

9. Sets are designed by the art director. ____

10. Set builders can re-create almost any setting on a sound stage. ____

11. However, many directors film on location instead. ____

12. A movie is given a look of realism by location filming. ____

13. Lighting electricians are called *gaffers* by others on the crew. ____

14. Lighting creates the proper mood for a scene. ____

15. At long last, the first lines are spoken by an actor. ____

A clapstick identifies each take of a scene.

Grab Bag

Part 2

Write *A* if the verb in the sentence is active. Write *P* if the verb in the sentence is passive. Then rewrite each passive voice sentence so the verb is in active voice.

16. A movie's director controls the filming process. ___ _____

_____

17. Movie scenes are shot out of order by the cinematographer. ___ _____

_____

18. The film is put together later by the director and the editor. ___ _____

_____

19. Actors are given the most attention by movie audiences. ___ _____

_____

20. Much of a movie's appeal is created by workers behind the scenes, however. ___

_____

_____

Part 3

Write a letter to match each filmmaking professional with the job that person does. Then write a sentence about the role that interests you most. Write your sentence in the active voice.

___ director   A. writes the dialogue
___ screenwriter   B. designs sets for movies
___ gaffer   C. works with lighting
___ art director   D. chooses actors for roles
___ casting director E. controls the filming process

_____

_____

_____

Name _____

Grab Bag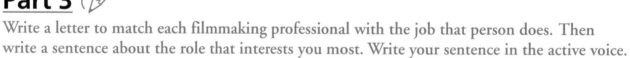

Read and Discover

a. Jackie Coogan was a famous child actor.

b. Jackie Coogan, a famous child actor, starred with Charlie Chaplin in *The Kid*.

Underline the phrase in sentence b. that tells who or what Jackie Coogan was. What punctuation marks separate this phrase from the rest of the sentence? _____

> An **appositive** is a phrase that identifies, or means the same thing as, a noun. Appositives follow the nouns they identify and are usually separated from the rest of a sentence by commas.

See Handbook Section 23

Part 1

Underline the appositive phrase in each sentence. Circle the noun it identifies.

1. Fans loved Shirley Temple, the most popular child star of the 1930s, for her curly hair and dimples.

2. Temple's special talents, singing and tap dancing, were highlighted in several musicals.

3. She wrote an autobiography, *Child Star*, in 1988.

Shirley Temple

4. Judy Garland, the star of *The Wizard of Oz*, first acted on stage at the age of four.

5. Garland changed her original name, Frances Gumm, when she began acting in movies.

6. Garland made the song, "Somewhere Over the Rainbow," the most popular song of all time.

7. She appeared with Mickey Rooney, another child star, in the *Andy Hardy* film series.

8. Garland's daughter, Liza Minelli, later became a movie star herself.

9. Tatum O'Neal won an Oscar, or Academy Award, when she was only ten.

10. She acted with her father, Ryan O'Neal, in *Paper Moon*.

11. *Home Alone*, a huge hit, made eleven-year-old Macaulay Culkin a star.

12. Culkin's character, a young boy accidentally left alone by his parents, must defend his home from burglars.

Part 2

Rewrite each pair of sentences as one sentence by changing the underlined section into an appositive.

13. <u>Liz Taylor was a child star.</u> Liz Taylor grew up to be a famous actress.

_____

_____

14. Ron Howard played the part of Opie on *The Andy Griffith Show*. <u>Ron Howard is a very successful movie director.</u>

_____

_____

15. Many child stars leave acting and work in other fields when they grow up. <u>Acting was their original profession.</u>

_____

_____

16. Shirley Temple became the ambassador to Ghana. <u>Ghana is a country in West Africa.</u>

_____

_____

Part 3

Identify each child star by reading the appositives. Use information from Parts 1 and 2 to help you. Write their names on the lines.

17. _____, star of the *Andy Hardy* series, acted with Judy Garland.

18. _____, author of *Child Star*, danced her way into America's

hearts in the 1930s.

19. _____, star of *Home Alone*, later acted in *My Girl*.

Name _____

Grab Bag

Read and Discover

   a. When a screenplay calls for imaginary events, filmmakers use special effects.

   b. Special effects have improved in recent years; movies are becoming much more realistic.

Cross out the comma in sentence a. and the semicolon in sentence b. Which sentence could become two separate sentences? _____

An **independent clause** is a sentence that makes sense by itself. A **compound sentence** is made of two closely related independent clauses. The two clauses can be joined by a comma and a conjunction (*and*, *but*, *or*) or by a semicolon (;). A **dependent clause** has a subject and a verb, but it does not make complete sense by itself. It needs an independent clause. A dependent clause begins with a subordinating conjunction such as *although, because, if, as,* or *when*. A **complex sentence** is made up of a dependent clause and an independent clause.

See Handbook Sections 8, 12, and 21

Part 1

Write *CD* next to each compound sentence and *CX* next to each complex sentence.

1. When directors made silent movies, they tried many special techniques. _____

2. Although some directors used fast motion, others turned the camera upside down. _____

3. The *matte shot* is a special effects technique; shots are blended into a single image. _____

4. If a director needed giant ants, he would film regular ants with a close-up lens. _____

5. Actors would run, and the director would film them against a blank background. _____

6. Technicians placed the film of the actors over the film of the ants; the illusion of giant ants was created. _____

7. If you see a chair move by itself, you are probably watching *stop-motion animation*. _____

8. Artists created a model of the chair, and they moved it slowly in front of a camera. _____

9. As the artists moved the model, cinematographers photographed it a few frames at a time. _____

10. When the film is played at regular speed, the model seems to move on its own. _____

Grab Bag

Part 2

Draw a line to match each clause on the left with a clause on the right. Write the new sentences on the lines. Be sure to use commas, semicolons, and periods correctly.

11. When computers came to Hollywood

12. Traditional special effects often looked fake

13. If filmmakers need dinosaurs in a movie

computer artists can create dinosaurs like the ones in <u>Jurassic Park</u>

they changed special effects completely

but computer effects can make almost anything look real

_____

_____

_____

_____

_____

Part 3

Pretend you are a special effects artist. Design and draw a creature for a science fiction movie. Then write one complex sentence describing your creature.

_____

_____

_____

Name _____

Grab Bag

Read  and Discover

Hollywood is a favorite tourist destination, movie fans from all over the world visit the area. Fun for the whole family. Tourists are people who go on trips to visit other places that are not their homes, and they go around touring these places to see all the sights that tourists want to see. Circle the phrase that has no verb. Underline the phrase that is made up of two independent clauses without a conjunction. Write *X* at the beginning of the phrase that uses a lot of words to say very little.

A **fragment** does not tell a complete thought. A **run-on sentence** is a compound sentence that is missing a comma and a conjunction. A **comma splice** is a run-on sentence that has a comma but is missing a conjunction. A **ramble-on** sentence is correct grammatically but contains extra words and phrases that don't add to its meaning. Avoid fragments, run-ons, comma splices, and ramble-ons in the final versions of your written work.

See Handbook Sections 13 and 21

Part 1 ✏️

Write *F* after each fragment. Write *RO* after each run-on. Write *CS* after each comma splice. Write *RA* after each ramble-on sentence.

1. Universal Studios is both a theme park and a working movie studio it is very popular. ___

2. Because visitors can go on rides based on famous movies. ___

3. Tours of the actual sets of movies and television shows. ___

4. One ride is based on the movie *E.T.*, on this ride visitors pedal bicycles to E.T.'s home. ___

5. *E.T.* is a very good movie in my opinion; I like it a lot because it is fun and enjoyable. ___

6. The Hollywood Studio Museum on Highland Avenue. ___

7. The museum building was a horse barn, it was later used as a silent movie studio. ___

8. Exhibits on the history of Hollywood movies. ___

9. Hollywood has a very interesting history, and many fascinating events involving famous people have happened in that glamorous town where movies are made. ___

10. Lucky tourists can sometimes see Hollywood history in action, some movie and TV scenes are shot on city streets near the studios. ___

Part 2 ✏️

Rewrite the sentences mentioned below from Part 1. Correct all fragments, run-ons, and comma splices. Shorten the ramble-ons. There is more than one way to correct each sentence. (11–15)

Sentence #1 _____

_____

Sentence #3 _____

_____

Sentence #6 _____

_____

Sentence #7 _____

_____

Sentence #9 _____

_____

Part 3 ✏️

This monster ramble-on sentence contains more than fifty words. See how short you can make it by crossing out unnecessary words, phrases, and clauses. Can you keep the main idea and make the sentence six words long?

Whenever the brilliant yellow sun shines on glittering Hollywood, which it does every day, you will find in that location many leisurely vacationing tourists who have come from other places and are there to visit, see, and experience the many sites and attractions of the area of Hollywood, that very wonderful town of magic.

Name _____

Grab Bag

Proofreading Others' Writing

Read this report about India's movie industry and find the mistakes. Use the proofreading marks below to show how each mistake should be fixed.

Proofreading Marks

Mark	Means	Example
ℒ	take away	Bombay, India, is ~~is~~ nicknamed "Bollywood."
∧	add	Bombay, India, _is_ nicknamed "Bollywood."
≡	make into a capital letter	Bombay, india, is nicknamed "Bollywood."
/	make into a lowercase letter	Bombay, India, is Nicknamed "Bollywood."
⊙	add a period	Bombay, India, is nicknamed "Bollywood"⊙
∧	add a comma	Bombay India, is nicknamed "Bollywood."
(sp)	fix spelling	Bombay, India, is nicknaimed "Bollywood."

"Bollywood"

Although Hollywood studios produce many movies. More movies are filmed in a a town nicknamed "Bollywood" in Bombay, india.

Bombay is the center of India's huge movie industry. India Produces more Feature Films than any other country. bombay lies on an island off the western coast of India it is India's largest city. Like Hollywood's climate. Bombay's climat is warm and sunny for most of the year.

Over 200 languages are spoken in India, most Bollywood movies are filmed in the Hindi language. Hindi, India's official language is one of the most widely spoken languages in the world.

Indian movies are packed with action other popular film are romances and stories of revenge.

Satyajit Ray one of India's famous directors, is known for his movies about the adventures of Apu. ray's movies show india, just after it had gained independence from British rule.

Movie tickets are inexpensive in India, films are the most popular forms of entertainment. With a population of over 900 million, India has has the world's largest movie audience.

Proofreading Your Own Writing

You can use the list below to help you find and fix mistakes in your own writing. Write the titles of your own stories or reports in the blanks on top of the chart. Then use the questions to check your work. Make a check mark (✓) in each box after you have checked that item.

Proofreading Checklist for Unit 1

	Titles			
Have I joined compound sentences correctly?				
Have I used complex sentences correctly?				
Have I avoided run-on sentences, comma splices, and fragments?				
Have I made sure that none of my sentences ramble on?				
Are most of my sentences in the active voice?				
Have I placed commas around each appositive?				

Also Remember . . .

Does each sentence begin with a capital letter?				
Have I spelled each word correctly?				
Have I used commas correctly?				

Your Own List
Use this space to write your own list of things to check in your writing.

Name _____

Grab Bag

Subjects and Predicates

Read each sentence and decide what its subject is. If the subject is understood *you*, write *you* on the line. Underline the complete subject. Draw a circle around the simple subject.

1. Gwilym Hughes has watched over 20,000 movies. _____

2. This film fan set a new world record. _____

3. Imagine his collection of ticket stubs! _____

Underline the complete predicate in each sentence. Draw a circle around the simple predicate.

4. Sydney Ling was the youngest director of a feature film.

5. He directed *Lex the Wonderdog* at the age of 13.

Draw one line under each compound subject in these sentences. Draw two lines under each compound predicate.

6. Richard Arlen and Walter Brennan began their film careers in unusual ways.

7. A film studio car hit Richard Arlen and broke his leg.

Complements and Prepositions

Decide whether the boldfaced word in each sentence is a direct object (DO), an indirect object (IO), a predicate noun (PN), or a predicate adjective (PA). Label each *DO, IO, PN,* or *PA* .

8. Walter Brennan was an **actor** in Hollywood. ___

9. He couldn't find **work**. ___

10. He was becoming **desperate**. ___

11. A movie director needed **help** with a stubborn donkey. ___

12. Brennan gave the **donkey** a voice. ___

13. Directors gave **Brennan** parts in many movies after that. ___

Underline the prepositional phrase in each sentence. Circle the preposition. Draw a box around its object.

14. *Die Zweite Heimat* is the longest movie of all time.

15. It lasts for 25 ½ hours.

Appositives

Underline the appositive in each sentence.

16. M. Maroof, a director in India, holds the record for shooting a film in the shortest time.

17. He shot a feature film, *Mohabbat Ka-Mashiba*, in two days.

Compound and Complex Sentences

Write *CD* next to each compound sentence. Write *CX* next to each complex sentence.

18. If a film is too long, the producers might cut some scenes. ____

19. "The Jitterbug" was a dance number in *The Wizard of Oz*, but the producers cut it out

of the movie. ____

20. The producers almost made a big mistake; they almost cut "Somewhere Over the

Rainbow," too! ____

Active and Passive Voice

Write *A* next to the sentence that is written in the active voice. Write *P* next to the sentence in the passive voice.

21. Sherlock Holmes has solved crimes in hundreds of movies. ____

22. This character has been played by at least 75 different actors. ____

Fragments, Run-ons, Comma Splices, Ramble-ons

Identify each item as a fragment (F), a run-on (RO), a comma splice (CS), or a ramble-on (RA). Label each *F, RO, CS,* or *RA.*

23. *Cleopatra* was the most expensive film ever made, its $44 million dollar budget would

cost over $200 million dollars today. ____

24. The story of the legendary queen of Egypt. ____

25. Elizabeth Taylor played Cleopatra she had 65 different costumes. ____

26. This lengthy movie is over four hours long, and that means that audiences must sit in

their seats for a very long time while they watch this movie until it is finally over. ____

Name _____

Grab Bag

FAMILY LEARNING OPPORTUNITIES

In Unit 1 of *G.U.M.* we are learning about different types of sentences and about the important parts of a sentence. The activities on this page give extra practice with some of the concepts we're learning. You can help reinforce the information your son or daughter is learning in school by choosing one or more activities to complete at home.

Take Two Eggs... (Simple Subjects, Simple Predicates; Understood *You*)

Invite your child to help you prepare your favorite easy dish. Ask your child to write down the recipe's steps as you go along. When the recipe is complete, have your child underline every sentence that has understood *you* as its simple subject. (Commands and requests have a subject of understood *you*. This means the subject, or doer of the action, is not named.)

Example	Crack two eggs into a bowl. ([You] crack two eggs into a bowl.)
	Beat the eggs well. ([You] beat the eggs well.)
	The beaten eggs should look smooth.
	Add a cup of flour. ([You] add a cup of flour.)
	The flour should be all-purpose flour.

Encourage your child to send the recipe to a friend or relative.

Kicked Around (Active and Passive Voice)

Ask your son or daughter to write a few sentences about a favorite sport from the point of view of the ball or puck. When your son or daughter finishes, work together to rewrite those sentences from the players' point of view.

Example	**Your child might write:**
	I was dribbled down the field by a halfback. (passive voice)
	I was kicked into the goal by the team's star player. (passive voice)
	And rewrite as:
	I dribbled the ball down the field. (active voice)
	I kicked the ball into the goal. (active voice)

As you rewrite the sentences, you will be changing some from the passive voice to the active voice. (In passive voice, the subject of a sentence has something done to it. In active voice, the subject of the sentence does something.) Encourage your child to write most of his or her sentences in active voice.

Grab Bag

What Would You Give? (Direct and Indirect Objects)

Invite your child to imagine that he or she had one million dollars to buy things for others. Have him or her write several sentences telling what he or she would give to whom. When the sentences are complete, ask your child to circle each indirect object and underline each direct object. (The direct object is the noun that receives the action of a verb. In this case it will be the gifts your child would give. The indirect object comes before the direct object. In this case it will be the people to whom your child would give the gifts.)

Example	I would give my (school) new lab equipment.

I would give my (friend) a new bicycle.

Where Is It? (Prepositional Phrases)

Ask your child to think of an object in your home and write several clues on a sheet of paper, telling where the object can be found but not naming the object. Encourage him or her to use prepositional phrases in the sentences. (Prepositional phrases begin with words such as *in, on, under, beside,* and *from*.) Then read the clues and try to guess what the object is.

Example	It's in the kitchen. It's on the counter. It's beside the stove. We toast bread in it.

Movie Crossword (Appositives)

Use the underlined phrases in each sentence to help you solve the clues with your child. (The underlined phrases are called *appositives*. An appositive follows a noun and identifies, or renames, the noun.) After you have completed the puzzle, work together to create your own movie crossword using the same kinds of clues. Underline appositives in the clues you write.

Across

2. __, a lovable bear, enjoys eating pots of honey.

4. __, the owner of a magic lamp, marries a princess.

7. __, a clever girl from Kansas, asks a wizard to send her back home.

Down

1. __, a Native American princess, brings peace between her people and the colonists.

3. __, a gentle killer whale, needs a friend's help to gain his freedom.

5. __, a mischievous round robot, helps Luke Skywalker on his mission.

6. __, a beautiful mermaid, falls in love with a human being.

Name _____

Grab Bag

Read and Discover

"**What** do *Apollo 13*, *Star Trek: Generations*, and *2001, A Space Odyssey* have in common?" asked Luna.

"**All** are movies set in space," replied Sol.

Circle the boldfaced word that asks a question. Underline the boldfaced word that refers to a group of people or things.

When the pronouns *who, whom, whose, which,* and *what* are used in questions, they are called **interrogative pronouns**. Use *who* as the subject of a clause or sentence. (*Who sent that E-mail message?*) Use *whom* as a direct or indirect object, or as the object of a preposition. (*For whom is that E-mail message?*) **Indefinite pronouns** refer to persons or things that are not identified as individuals. Indefinite pronouns include *all, anybody, both, either, anything, everyone, few, most, one, no one, several, nobody,* and *someone*.

See Handbook Sections 16 and 29

Part 1

Circle each boldfaced interrogative pronoun in the paragraphs below. Underline each boldfaced indefinite pronoun. (1–11)

"*Apollo 13* was based on the book *Lost Moon*. By **whom** was it written?" Stella asked.

"I know!" shouted Neil. "It was written by Jim Lovell, commander of the *Apollo 13* moon mission. Now I have a question for you: **who** co-wrote that book with Jim Lovell?" **Nobody** knew the answer to Neil's question, so he revealed that Jeffrey Kluger was the co-author.

Stella asked her friends if they had seen *Apollo 13*. **Several** said they had. "**Which** would you rather watch," Stella asked, "a videotape of *Apollo 13* or one of *2001, A Space Odyssey?*"

The flight of *Apollo 13* nearly ended in tragedy.

"**What** are the plots?" asked Leo. **Someone** explained that *2001, A Space Odyssey* is about a computer that tries to take over a spacecraft, while *Apollo 13* is the story of a failed space mission.

"Does **anybody** remember **who** starred in *Apollo 13?*" asked Leo.

"Tom Hanks, Kevin Bacon, and Bill Paxton," Luna said. Many people have good memories, but **few** have memories as good as hers.

Part 2 ✏️

Complete each sentence by writing a pronoun from the word bank. Remember to capitalize a word that begins a sentence.

| whom | everything | who | everyone | no one | several | something | which |

12. "_____ knows the name of the actor who played Captain Kirk on *Star Trek*?" asked Neil.

13. "William Shatner, of course," said Luna. "Now ask me _____ I don't know."

14. "You know _____," said Stella.

15. Their friends were amused. _____ laughed.

16. "Here's a question about *Apollo 13*," said Neil. "For _____ was Jack Swigert substituting on the *Apollo 13* mission?"

17. _____ knew the answer, so Neil told them that astronaut Ken Mattingly was grounded by the measles.

18. Then Neil said, "Either Ed Harris or Gary Sinise played Ken Mattingly in *Apollo 13*. _____ was it?"

"Gary Sinise, of course," said Luna.

Part 3 ✏️

Write two trivia questions about your favorite movie. Use interrogative pronouns. You might want to challenge a friend to answer them.

_____

_____

_____

Name _____

The World Outside

Read  and Discover

The sun **is** an ordinary star. Ninety per cent of the stars we **can see** from Earth are *main-sequence* stars like our sun.

Which boldfaced verb connects a noun with a phrase that describes it? _____ Which boldfaced verb shows action? _____

> An **action verb** shows action. A **linking verb** does not show action. Instead, a linking verb connects the subject of a sentence to a word(s) that describes or renames the subject. Linking verbs are usually forms of *be*. Common linking verbs include *am, is, are, was, were,* and *will be*. The verbs *become, seem, appear,* and *look* can also be used as linking verbs.

See Handbook Section 17

Part 1

Circle each action verb. Underline each linking verb. Be sure to include helping verbs such as *can, would, may,* and *have*.

1. Scientists observe stars as tiny as 12 miles in diameter and as big as a billion miles in diameter.

2. The sun is about 4.6 billion years old.

3. The average age of a star is between one million and ten billion years.

4. Stars can last as long as 15 billion years.

5. A star begins its life as a cloud of hydrogen gas and dust.

6. Hydrogen, the lightest chemical element, is highly flammable.

7. Over millions of years, the cloud's gravity pulls it into a ball.

8. The ball's center becomes extremely hot.

9. Temperatures of two million degrees Fahrenheit result in nuclear fusion.

10. Fusion slowly changes the hydrogen in the ball's center into helium.

11. Helium is a very light, unburnable gas.

12. Nuclear fusion releases energy.

13. The ball's outer layer becomes heated.

14. Then the newborn star shines.

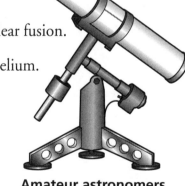

Amateur astronomers watch the stars through telescopes.

The World Outside

Part 2

Write an action verb or a linking verb from the word bank to complete each sentence correctly.

Linking verbs	Action verbs
is	explodes
are	revolve
can be	changes

15. Stars _____ blue, white, yellow, orange, or red.

16. Blue stars _____ hotter than red ones.

17. The two stars in a *binary star* _____ around each other.

18. A *white dwarf* _____ a small, dense star that is very hot

and bright for its size.

19. A *main-sequence star* _____ into a *red giant* when its

supply of hydrogen decreases.

20. A *supernova* _____ suddenly, becoming billions of

times brighter than before.

Part 3

Circle three action verbs and three linking verbs in the puzzle. Then write each verb in the correct column.

K	B	C	S	Q	U	P	W
A	E	X	P	L	O	D	E
R	C	M	Q	V	M	T	R
E	O	B	S	E	R	V	E
L	M	R	F	P	G	C	H
S	E	A	R	C	H	V	B

Linking Verbs

21. _____

22. _____

23. _____

Action Verbs

24. _____

25. _____

26. _____

Name _____

The World Outside

Read and Discover

Perhaps in the future the U.S. space program **will discover** life-bearing planets in other solar systems. NASA administrator Daniel Goldin **made** this prediction. The idea of life on other planets **excites** some people and **frightens** others.

Circle the boldfaced verb that tells about something that is going to happen. Underline the boldfaced verb that tells about something that has already happened. Draw a box around two boldfaced verbs that tell about something that happens regularly or is true now.

A **present-tense verb** is used to indicate that something happens regularly or is true now. A **past-tense verb** tells about something that has already happened. Regular verbs form the past tense by adding -*ed*. Irregular verbs change their spelling in the past tense. A **future-tense verb** tells what is going to happen. Add the helping verb *will* to the present-tense form of a verb to form the future tense. **Remember to use this information when you speak, too**.

See Handbook Section 17

Part 1

Circle each present-tense verb. Underline each past-tense verb. Draw a box around each future-tense verb. If the helping verb is separated from the main verb, box each verb separately.

1. In 1994, radio astronomers examined signals from a pulsar, or dead star.

2. These scientists found the first evidence of planets outside our solar system.

3. Two or three planets orbit that pulsar.

4. Maybe the scientists will confirm the number soon.

5. Probably nothing lives on those planets; their environments contain too much radiation.

6. In October 1995, two Swiss astronomers reported another exciting finding.

7. Very close to 51 Pegasi, a sunlike star, they found a planet about half as big as Jupiter.

8. Scientists probably will not discover life on this planet, either.

9. Its proximity to its parent star makes it too hot.

10. Scientists study the far reaches of the universe every day.

11. Soon they will have technology for analysis of the atmospheres of distant planets.

The World Outside

Part 2

Decide which tense of the verb in parentheses should be used in each sentence. Write the verb in the correct tense. Add a helping verb if you need one.

12. Recently, two California astronomers _____ 120 sunlike stars over

    a period of eight years. (observe)

13. Their perseverance finally _____ off. (pay)

14. In their study, two stars—70 Virginis and 47 Ursa Majoris— _____

    wobbling motions. (reveal)

15. This kind of motion usually _____ the gravitational pull of planets

    much larger than Jupiter. (suggest)

16. In the future you probably _____ more about these two astronomers, Dr.

    Geoffrey Marcy and Dr. Paul Butler. (hear)

Part 3

Write a memo to Dr. Marcy and Dr. Butler. Tell them whether you think they will discover extraterrestrial life. If you like, thank them for their work. Use at least one present-tense verb, one past-tense verb, and one future-tense verb.

M E M O

DATE: _____

TO: Dr. Geoffrey Marcy and Dr. Paul Butler

FROM: _____

RE: Extraterrestrials

_____

_____

_____

Name _____

Read  and Discover

Because Mercury, Venus, Mars, Jupiter, and Saturn are easily visible to the naked eye, people **have known** of these five planets since ancient times. The planet Uranus was discovered in 1781. Astronomers **had seen** Uranus before then, but they **had believed** it was a star.
Circle the boldfaced verb that tells about an action that began in the past and continues today. Underline the two boldfaced verbs that tell about actions that were definitely completed in the past.

The **present perfect** tense shows action that started in the past and was recently completed or is still happening. To form the present perfect tense, add the helping verb *has* or *have* to the past participle of a verb (*have known*). The **past perfect** tense shows action that was definitely completed in the past. To form the past perfect tense, add the helping verb *had* to the past participle of a verb (*had believed*).
Remember to use this information when you speak, too.

See Handbook Section 17

Part 1

Circle the boldfaced verbs that are in the present perfect tense. Underline the boldfaced verbs that are in the past perfect tense. (1–14)

The planet Neptune was discovered in September 1846. Before then, no one **had known** that it existed. Earlier that year, astronomers in Germany **had received** information from a French mathematician, Urbain J.J. Leverrier. He **had figured** out that Uranus's orbit was probably being affected by the gravity of an unknown planet. Leverrier **had predicted** where that unknown planet would be at a certain time. Astronomers used his figures and by September **had found** Neptune.

We **have known** that there are nine planets in our solar system since 1930, when Clyde W. Tombaugh discovered the outermost planet, Pluto. Astronomers **had noticed** irregularities in Neptune's orbit, and this **had led** to the discovery of another planet.

Scientists believe that we **have found** all of the planets in our solar system. Some scientists **have continued** the search for another planet orbiting the sun. They **have called** this planet "Planet X."

Various scientists **have guessed** how big Planet X is. They **have suggested** that it is three to five times as big as Earth. They **have speculated** that it takes 1,000 years to orbit the sun.

Part 2

Write the present perfect form (*has* or *have* and past participle) or the past perfect form (*had* and past participle) of the verb in parentheses to complete each sentence correctly.

15. Since ancient times people _____ curious about the other planets. (be)

16. Recently, NASA _____ many unmanned space flights to collect

     information about the planets. (launch)

17. Some of the ships that _____ our solar system include the *Mariner* and

     Viking spacecrafts, the *Pioneer* probes, and *Voyagers 1* and *2*. (explore)

18. Between 1977 and 1989, *Voyager 2* was able to fly near Jupiter, Saturn, Uranus, and

     Neptune because these giant planets _____ up in perfect order. (line)

19. The last time this _____ was 175 years earlier! (happen)

20. By the time *Voyager 2* visited Neptune, it _____ almost five billion

     miles in twelve years! (travel)

Part 3

Imagine you are the driver of a space taxi that transports people between Earth and the other planets of our solar system. Write a few sentences telling about a typical workday. Use at least two perfect tense verbs.

_____

_____

_____

_____

_____

_____

Name _____

The World Outside

44
G.U.M.

Read and Discover

I **am watching** a tape of the first moon walk. My mom was my age in 1969 when everyone **was talking** about that event. When I celebrate my fiftieth birthday, my children **will be planning** a trip to the moon. Circle the boldfaced verb phrase that tells about an action that is going on now. Underline the boldfaced verb phrase that tells about an action that was happening in the past. Draw a box around the verb phrase that tells about an action that will happen in the future.

Verbs in **progressive tenses** show continuing action. To form the **present progressive** tense, add *am, is,* or *are* to the present participle of a verb. (*I am eating.*) To form the **past progressive** tense, add *was* or *were* to the present participle. (*They were eating.*) To form the **future progressive** tense, add *will be* to the present participle. (*You will be eating.*)

See Handbook Section 17

Part 1

Read each sentence. If it contains a progressive tense form, write *P* on the line. Write *X* if the boldfaced verb is not in a progressive tense.

1. I **am reading** a book about the first moon walk. ____

2. I **have started** a report on this topic. ____

3. During the 1960s, both the United States and the Soviet Union **were improving** their space programs. ____

4. In 1964 Americans were concerned because the Soviets **had become** the first to send a human being on a space walk. ____

5. By June, the U.S. **had sent** its own astronaut to walk in space, Edward H. White II. ____

6. By December 1968, *Apollo 8* **had orbited** the moon. ____

7. The U.S. **was coming** close to its goal of landing people safely on the moon. ____

8. Imagine that it is July 1969 and you **are waiting** with astronauts Aldrin, Armstrong, and Collins inside the command module of *Apollo 11.* ____

9. People all over the world **are watching** the thrilling event on television. ____

10. Soon you **will be hopping** on the moon. ____

Apollo 11's lunar module landed on the moon.

Part 2

Use a helping verb from the word bank plus a form of the verb in parentheses to complete each sentence correctly. Each verb you write should be in a progressive tense.

	is	are	am	were	will be

11. In the 1960s, the United States and the Soviet Union _____

    against each other to make new discoveries. (compete)

12. Today, Russian and American astronauts _____ together to

    explore space. (work)

13. Maybe someday Russians and Americans _____ together on

    Mars. (stand)

14. I _____ about becoming an astronaut myself. (think)

15. Maybe someday I _____ inside a spacecraft, listening to some-

    one saying "We have lift-off!" (sit)

Part 3

Complete the clues by writing the present progressive tense form of the verb in parentheses.
Use the clues to solve the riddle.

If you (sit) _____ down, I'm the one who's keeping you in your chair.

If you (stand) _____ up, I'm the reason you're not floating in air.

When astronauts (bounce) _____ around,

I (feel) _____ too weak to keep them down.

So if you (wish) _____ you could swim through the air,

You should travel in space, Because I'm not there.

What am I? ___ ___ ___ ___ ___ ___ ___

Name _____

The World Outside

Read  and Discover

Black holes have been portrayed as **incredibly horrible** monsters. Circle the boldfaced word that describes a noun. Draw a box around the boldfaced word that tells about an adjective.

Adjectives describe nouns and pronouns. Some adjectives tell what kind. Others, like *many* and *six*, tell how many. The adjectives *this, that, these,* and *those* tell which one. These words are called *demonstrative adjectives*. The articles *a, an,* and *the* are also adjectives. **Adverbs** describe verbs or adjectives. They tell how, when, where, or to what extent (how much). Many adverbs end in *-ly*. Other common adverbs are *fast, very, often, again, only, however, too, later, first, then, far, still,* and *now*.

See Handbook Sections 15 and 18

Part 1

Circle each boldfaced word that is an adjective. Draw a star above each boldfaced adjective that is an article. Draw a box around each boldfaced word that is an adverb.

1. The **menacing** black hole lurks unseen in space.

2. **There** it sits **patiently**, waiting to gobble up unsuspecting flying objects.

3. It sucks **innocent** stars, comets, and spheres into the **deadly** whirlpool of its gravity.

4. This is how black holes form: **a** new star changes **slowly**.

5. After millions of years, its supply of hydrogen dwindles **substantially**.

6. A **large** star uses up its supply of hydrogen more quickly than a **small** star.

7. When its hydrogen is **almost** gone, a star becomes a *red giant*.

8. A star the size of our sun will **finally** become a **small**, hot *white dwarf*.

9. A star that is more than **three** times the size of our sun becomes a *supergiant*.

10. It may **then** become a *supernova*.

11. A supernova is an **extremely** large exploding star.

12. If there is **still** a **large** amount of mass left over after a supernova explodes, **the** star collapses

    into itself and forms a black hole.

The World Outside

Part 2

Fill in each blank with an adjective or an adverb. Use words from the word bank or your own words. Then circle each adverb you wrote. (13–19)

| three | incredibly | strange | black | there | huge | invisible |

In 1994, the Hubble Space Telescope discovered something _____

and _____ at the core of galaxy M87. A giant _____

hole had formed _____. A black hole is _____ to

the human eye. It appears black because it swallows light. Only stars that are more than

_____ times as large as our sun can become black holes. A black hole's

gravity is _____ strong.

Part 3

Circle four adverbs and four adjectives in the puzzle. Then write each word in the correct column.

M	A	N	Y	R	K	B	T	I
B	P	W	B	Q	G	D	H	N
N	Q	D	T	H	I	S	F	V
T	H	E	J	M	X	L	K	I
H	C	Q	A	L	W	A	Y	S
E	G	F	V	K	Z	H	W	I
R	M	S	T	R	O	N	G	B
E	G	L	D	J	C	S	K	L
E	X	T	R	E	M	E	L	Y

Adjectives

20. _____

21. _____

22. _____

23. _____

Adverbs

24. _____

25. _____

26. _____

27. _____

Name _____

The World Outside

Read and Discover

Wow, the air is so clear today! I can see **across** the valley.
Which boldfaced word begins a phrase that tells *where?* _____
Which boldfaced word expresses emotion? _____

A **preposition** shows a relationship between one word in a sentence and the noun or pronoun that follows the preposition. This noun or pronoun is called the **object of the preposition**. The preposition, the object of the preposition, and the words in between them make a **prepositional phrase**. An **interjection** expresses emotion. *Oh, ouch, hey, hurray,* and *wow* are common interjections.

See Handbook Sections 19 and 22

Part 1

In the sentences below, underline each prepositional phrase. Circle the preposition and draw a box around its object. Draw a star above each interjection.

1. Scientists have divided Earth's atmosphere into four layers.

2. We live in the *troposphere,* the layer closest to Earth.

3. Wow, the troposphere can be a stormy place: most of Earth's weather conditions occur inside it.

4. The layer above the troposphere is called the *stratosphere.*

5. Oh, here's something I didn't know: most airline pilots fly in the stratosphere so they can avoid bad weather.

6. The stratosphere ends thirty miles above Earth's surface.

7. Most of Earth's ozone is in the stratosphere.

8. Ozone in the stratosphere shields us from ultraviolet sunrays.

9. The *mesosphere,* the third layer of our atmosphere, ends fifty miles above Earth.

10. It is cold in the mesosphere; gas trails left by meteors can be seen there.

11. The outermost and thickest layer of our atmosphere is the *thermosphere.*

12. The air in the thermosphere is completely exposed to the sun's radiation.

13. This can cause Fahrenheit temperatures of 3600 degrees. Ouch, that's hot!

Auroral display	120 mi. (200 km)
Thermosphere	
	50 mi. (80 km)
Mesosphere	
Meteor trails	
	30 mi. (48 km)
Ozone layer	
Stratosphere	
	10 mi. (16 km)
Troposphere	

The World Outside

Part 2 ✎

Write a prepositional phrase from the word bank to complete each sentence correctly.

of human health problems with natural substances	in 1905 into the air	over London

14. The term *smog* was first used _____.

15. The word was invented to describe the smoky fog that hung _____

_____.

16. Automobiles and other human inventions release harmful chemicals _____

_____.

17. These chemicals combine _____

to create dangerous ozone.

18. Smog ozone is a major cause _____.

Part 3 ✎

Imagine it is the year 2017. As a result of strong clean-air laws, the use of nonpolluting vehicles, and cleaner fuels, air pollution is almost nonexistent! Write a journal entry telling how you feel about this. Use at least one interjection. Underline each prepositional phrase you use.

_____

_____

_____

_____

_____

_____

Name _____

The World Outside

Read  and Discover

Venus **and** Mars are Earth's closest neighbors. Mars's atmosphere is more like Earth's than any other planet's, **but** Martian air is still very different from ours. **If** scientists could change the Martian atmosphere, people might be able to live on Mars.

Which boldfaced word links two proper nouns? _____

Which boldfaced word links two independent clauses? _____

Which boldfaced word begins a dependent clause? _____

Coordinating conjunctions (*and*, *but*, *or*) connect words or groups of words (including independent clauses) that are similar. **Subordinating conjunctions,** such as *although*, *because*, *since*, *so*, *if*, and *before*, show how one clause is related to another. Subordinating conjunctions are used at the beginning of dependent clauses.

See Handbook Section 21

Part 1

Underline each coordinating conjunction. Circle each subordinating conjunction.

1. Mars is about half the size of Earth and twice the size of our moon.

2. Since Mars rotates once about every 24 hours, a day on Mars is the same length as Earth's.

3. Because Mars's orbit takes 687 days, the Martian year is almost twice as long as Earth's.

4. Like Earth, Mars is tilted on its axis, so it has seasonal changes.

5. Mars has weaker gravity, a thinner atmosphere, and colder temperatures than Earth.

6. If you weigh 100 pounds on Earth, you would weigh about 38 pounds on Mars.

7. Because Mars's atmosphere is extremely thin, it cannot hold heat very well.

8. There is not enough oxygen on Mars for people to breathe, and it is often incredibly cold.

9. Daytime temperatures on Mars are sometimes similar to those on Earth, but nighttime temperatures plunge to minus 125° F.

10. Although Mars has little water today, scientists believe it once had lakes and rivers.

11. Apparently there is some water trapped in polar ice caps on Mars, and there are deep canyons that were probably carved by water.

The World Outside

Part 2

Complete each sentence with a conjunction from the word bank. Capitalize a conjunction that begins a sentence.

so	if	or	and	but	although

12. To make Mars habitable for people, scientists would need to create an atmosphere with a combination of carbon dioxide, oxygen, _____ water vapor.

13. Mars has all the resources necessary for this to happen, _____ one day people might walk on Mars without space suits.

14. _____ scientists pump gases called *fluorocarbons* into the Martian atmosphere, it could create a "greenhouse effect."

15. _____ fluorocarbons have had a negative effect on Earth's atmosphere, they might improve the Martian atmosphere.

16. This idea may sound strange, _____ some scientists believe it might work: giant mirrors could be launched to reflect sunlight to melt Mars's ice caps.

17. It might take less than 200 years to *terraform* Mars's atmosphere, _____ make it more like Earth's.

Part 3

Draw something you might find in a human colony on Mars. You might draw a map of the colony, a Martian room, or a Martian vehicle. Write one sentence to describe your picture. Use at least one subordinating or coordinating conjunction.

_____

_____

_____

Name _____

The World Outside

Proofreading Others' Writing

Read this report about constellations and find the mistakes. Use the proofreading marks below to show how each mistake should be corrected.

Proofreading Marks

Mark	Means	Example
℈	take away	Groups of of stars are called *constellations*.
∧	add	Groups of stars are called *constellations*.
≡	make into a capital letter	groups of stars are called *constellations*.
⊙	add a period	Groups of stars are called *constellations*⊙
/	make into a lowercase letter	Groups of stars are called /Constellations.
(sp)	fix spelling	Groups of stars are called *constelations*.

Constellations

Ancient peoples such as the Romans saw pictures in the night sky formed by groupings of Stars. They named most of these groupings, or *constellations,* after animals or mythological characters, and they told stories about why they're gods had placed the constellations in the sky. Family relationships exist among many of the constellations. For instance, the constellation Andromeda is near her husband, Perseus, and also is near her parents, Cassiopeia and cepheus.

By who was Andromeda placed in the sky? The goddess Athene placed her there to reward andromeda for her loyalty to Perseus.

Perseus had fallen in love with Andromeda Her was chained to a rock, about to be eaten by a monster. This monster will be closing in on her when Perseus killed it and unchained Andromeda.

Perseus wasn't no stranger to monsters. Earlier he has killed the Gorgon Medusa. medusa was incredible dangerous! When people looked at herself, they turned to stone.

Today, astronomers used the constellations as markers in the sky. The star 51 Pegasi got its name from its location in the constellasion Pegasus, the flying horse.

Proofreading Your Own Writing

You can use the list below to help you find and fix mistakes in your own writing. Write the titles of your own stories or reports in the blanks on top of the chart. Then use the questions to check your work. Make a check mark (✓) in each box after you have checked that item.

Proofreading Checklist for Unit 2

	Titles			
Have I capitalized proper nouns and used plural and possessive nouns correctly?				
Have I used personal, compound personal, possessive, interrogative, and indefinite pronouns correctly?				
Have I used adverbs and adjectives correctly?				
Have I used progressive and perfect tenses correctly?				
Have I used prepositions and interjections correctly?				
Have I used coordinating and subordinating conjunctions correctly?				

Also Remember . . .

Does each sentence begin with a capital letter?				
Does each sentence end with the right mark?				
Have I spelled each word correctly?				
Have I used commas correctly?				

Your Own List
Use this space to write your own list of things to check in your writing.

Name _____

The World Outside

Nouns and Pronouns

Circle the boldfaced noun that is a proper noun. Underline the boldfaced noun that is plural. Draw a box around the boldfaced noun that is possessive.

1. On *Star Trek*, DeForest Kelley played the **ship's** doctor, McCoy.

2. Nichelle Nichols played the part of **Uhura.**

3. One of her **jobs** was to communicate with other spacecrafts.

Rewrite each sentence. Replace each boldfaced word or phrase with a pronoun.

4. George Takei played Sulu; **Sulu** sat near Captain Kirk on the bridge. _____

   _____

5. Captain Kirk often seemed to be talking to **Captain Kirk,** but he was actually recording a

   log of the ship activities. _____

   _____

6. I wonder what **Kelley's, Nichols's, and Takei's** conversations with their friends were like

   when they were relaxing after work. _____

   _____

Read each question and answer. Complete each question by writing an interrogative or an indefinite pronoun from the word bank.

whose	anyone	who

7. _____ played Captain Picard in *Star Trek: The Next Generation*? Patrick

   Stewart played the starship captain.

8. _____ ears are *Star Trek* fans imitating when they wear pointed plastic ears?

   Mr. Spock's Vulcan ears, of course.

9. Does _____ know who Gene Roddenberry was? He created the original *Star*

   Trek series.

The World Outside

G.U.M.

Verbs

Circle each boldfaced action verb. Underline each boldfaced linking verb.

10. Polaris, which is in the constellation Ursa Minor, **is** the North Star.

11. Sailors **have navigated** by the North Star for centuries.

Circle the word or phrase in parentheses that identifies the tense of each boldfaced verb.

12. NASA doctors **study** the effects of space travel on human beings. (present/future)

13. In the future people **will be staying** in space for longer periods. (perfect/progressive)

14. Between 1958 and 1961, monkeys **flew** in several NASA space missions. (past/past perfect)

15. Because the monkeys **had done** well in space, it was considered safe to send up humans.

    (past/past perfect)

16. Today's NASA doctors **are continuing** their studies in this field. (perfect/progressive)

Adjectives and Adverbs

Circle the boldfaced words that are adjectives. Put a box around each boldfaced adjective that is an article. Underline the boldfaced words that are adverbs.

17. The **powerful** telescope stood **alone** on **a** Hawaiian mountaintop.

18. **The** spectators who gathered **there** said that the **solar** eclipse was **amazingly** beautiful.

Prepositions and Interjections

Underline the prepositional phrases. Circle each preposition and draw a box around its object. Draw a star above each interjection.

19. Wow, Earth's shadow is sliding over the moon!

20. The shadow has changed the moon's whiteness to a dark red.

Conjunctions

Circle each coordinating conjunction. Underline each subordinating conjunction.

21. Since archaeoastronomy brings together several fields, astronomers, archaeologists, and

    other specialists may work together.

22. Although they had no telescopes, ancient peoples made accurate observations of the stars.

Name _____

The World Outside

FAMILY LEARNING OPPORTUNITIES

In Unit 2 of *G.U.M.* we are studying the eight parts of speech: nouns, pronouns, verbs, adjectives, adverbs, prepositions, conjunctions, and interjections. The activities on these pages give extra practice with some of the concepts we're learning. You can help reinforce the lessons your son or daughter is learning in school by choosing one or more activities to complete together at home.

Crossword Puzzle (Personal, Compound, Possessive Pronouns)

Work with your child to solve the puzzle. The answers are compound personal pronouns. (Compound personal pronouns contain the word *self* or *selves.* They include *myself, himself, themselves,* and *ourselves,* among others.)

Across

1. I looked at __ in the mirror.
3. We packed a picnic lunch for __.
4. They laughed at __ in their funny costumes.
6. She was surprised at __ for being frightened by the fly.

Down

2. You should be proud of __.
5. He is proud of __ for finishing the project.

Interstellar Survey (Personal, Compound, Possessive Pronouns)

Help your child conduct a survey. Together, write the name of each family member on a sheet of paper. (Include friends and neighbors if you like.) Have your son or daughter ask each person on the list how soon, if ever, he or she thinks we will: 1) send humans to explore the moon further; 2) land humans on Mars; and 3) discover extraterrestrial life. Ask your son or daughter to record each person's answers and to report the results to you in complete sentences. Have your child identify each personal pronoun, compound personal pronoun, and possessive pronoun he or she uses. (Personal pronouns include *I, he, she, it, you, me, they,* and *them.* Compound personal pronouns include *himself* and *herself.* Possessive pronouns include *my, his, her, our,* and *their.*)

Example	**Our** cousin Ross thinks **we** should build a space station on the moon. **He** volunteers **himself** as one of the first settlers there.

The Gnu's Shoes Were Blue (Kinds of Nouns)

You can play this game with the whole family. Give each person two index cards. Invite each person to write two nouns. (A noun names a person, place, thing, or idea.) One noun should be singular (*fox*) and one should be plural (*foxes*). Combine the index cards into one pile. Form teams of two players and take turns selecting two cards from the pile. Each team then has one minute to come up with a sentence that includes both nouns and uses one of them as a possessive. (Possessive nouns, such as *child's* and *children's*, show ownership.) Encourage teams to make their sentences as silly as possible.

Example	The **fox** took the **child's** hat.

Yesterday, Today, and Tomorrow (The Present, Past, Future Tenses)

Look through old magazines with your son or daughter to find photographs of people performing ordinary duties such as doing laundry or cooking dinner. Cut out one of these photos. Then have your son or daughter draw two pictures to go with it. One picture should show someone doing the same activity 100 years ago, and the other should show someone doing it 100 years in the future. Ask your son or daughter to write a caption to go with each picture. One caption should be in the past tense, one should be in the present tense, and the third should be in the future tense.

Example	1. In the past people **heated** water on stoves, **washed** clothes in tubs, and **hung** them on clotheslines to dry.

   2. Today we **wash** clothes in washing machines and **dry** them in dryers.

   3. In the future all clothes **will be cleaned** in seconds by a nonpolluting process called "InstaClean." People **will walk** into the nearest InstaClean booth, and their clothes **will become** clean in a flash!

Mars Is Cold, Red, and Dry (Coordinating and Subordinating Conjunctions)

Work with your son or daughter to research a planet in our solar system, or choose another topic related to the atmosphere or to outer space. Have your son or daughter write six short sentences about the topic. Then work together to see how many pairs of sentences you can combine. You can use coordinating conjunctions (*and, or, but*) or subordinating conjunctions (*since, because, if, although*).

Example	Venus is the second planet from the sun. It is about the same size as Earth. It is too hot to support life.

   Venus is the same size as Earth, **but** it is too hot to support life.

Name _____

Read  and Discover

There is a bee on **your** collar. Look out! **You're** going to be stung! Circle the boldfaced word that means "you are." Underline the boldfaced word that shows ownership.

The words **your** and **you're** sound alike but have different spellings and meanings. *Your* is a possessive pronoun and shows ownership. *You're* is a contraction made from the words *you* and *are*.

See Handbook Section 30

Part 1

Read this conversation. Circle a word in parentheses to complete each sentence correctly. (1–15)

"Hello, Mr. Garcia! Are (your/you're) bees making honey?" asked Mina.

"Yes, they are. I'll bring a jar to you and (your/you're) family tomorrow," Mr. Garcia answered. "(Your/You're) interested in beekeeping, aren't you?"

"Yes. Can you tell me how (your/you're) bees make honey?"

"They gather nectar from flowers, such as the roses in (your/you're) yard," Mr. Garcia said. "The bees add proteins to the nectar. As the nectar evaporates, it turns into honey."

"Does the whole hive really work together?" Mina asked.

As bees gather nectar, they also help pollinate flowers.

"(Your/You're) exactly right," Mr. Garcia answered. "Each bee has a special job to do."

"(Your/You're) work sounds interesting!" Mina said.

Mr. Garcia said, "If (your/you're) really curious, you can help me work with my bees."

"I'd love to see (your/you're) beehives," replied Mina. "Is it true that (your/you're) supposed to wear a special suit with gloves and a veil?"

"(Your/You're) right," he said. "If you don't protect (your/you're) skin, the bees can sting you."

"(Your/You're) going to have to help me convince my parents that I will be safe," Mina said.

"If (your/you're) careful to do as I say, you will be perfectly safe," Mr. Garcia said. "I'll talk with (your/you're) parents tomorrow," he added.

Beasts & Critters

Part 2

Write *your* or *you're* on each blank to correctly complete each sentence. Remember to capitalize a word that begins a sentence.

16. "Do 50,000 bees really live on _____ farm, Jamal?" asked Noemi.

17. "There must be a lot of flowers near _____ house," she continued.

18. "_____ right," said Jamal. "A colony of bees can collect up to 15 pounds of nectar in one day."

19. "I hope _____ going to tell me more," Noemi said.

20. "If you were a bee and you stung someone while defending _____ hive, you would die soon afterwards," Jamal said.

21. "_____ really an expert!" Noemi said.

22. "Thanks for sharing _____ knowledge," she continued.

23. "_____ welcome," said Jamal.

24. "If _____ not busy, maybe we could talk more about bees tomorrow," Noemi suggested.

Part 3

Pretend you are a beekeeper. Invite a friend to visit your beehives. Tell your friend what he or she will see. Use *your* and *you're* correctly.

_____

_____

_____

_____

_____

Name _____

Beasts & Critters

Read  and Discover

"Look at the fireflies over **there**. **They're** glowing!" Andrey said.
"They use **their** ability to glow to attract mates," replied Mara.

Which boldfaced word means "belonging to them"? _____

Which boldfaced word means "they are"? _____

Which boldfaced word means "in that place"? _____

The words *their, there,* and *they're* sound almost the same but have different meanings and spellings. *Their* is a possessive pronoun and means "belonging to them." *There* is an adverb and means "in that place." *There* may also be used as an introductory word. *They're* is a contraction that means "they are."

See Handbook Section 30

Part 1

Circle the word in parentheses that correctly completes each sentence.

1. (Their/There/They're) are about 1,900 different species of fireflies.

2. (Their/There/They're) a kind of beetle; sometimes they are called "lightning bugs."

3. Adult fireflies can tell whether another firefly is one of (their/there/they're) own kind when it flashes its signal.

4. Fireflies aren't the only creatures that glow. Some bacteria and fish share (their/there/they're) ability to give off light.

A chemical reaction in fireflies' bodies produces light.

5. New Zealand glowworms also give off light; (their/there/they're) related to the housefly.

6. Glowworms make sticky, glowing threads that they use to catch (their/there/they're) food.

7. (Their/There/They're) are a number of uses for light-producing creatures.

8. In some places, people catch fireflies in transparent containers and use the containers as lanterns to light (their/there/they're) way.

9. Scientists have used the gene that makes fireflies glow to test (their/there/they're) medicines.

10. Look at the fireflies over (their/there/they're).

11. (Their/There/They're) glinting in between the trees.

12. (Their/There/They're) entire bodies seem to glow.

Part 2

Write *their*, *there*, or *they're* to complete each sentence correctly. Remember to capitalize a word that begins a sentence.

13. "I see some fireflies over _____!" said Max.

14. "_____ really making a lot of light!" Katya observed.

15. "Now _____ all beginning to flash at the same time," Max noticed.

16. "Which part of _____ bodies gives off light?" he asked.

17. "Most fireflies have light organs on the bottom side of _____ abdomens," answered Katya.

18. "Is it true that _____ only going to live for a few days?" Max asked.

19. "Once _____ adults, fireflies only live five to thirty days," Katya said.

20. "Do you think they will lay _____ eggs in that tree?" Max wondered.

21. "No, they won't lay them _____," Katya responded.

22. "_____ going to lay them on or in the ground."

Part 3

Write three or four questions you have about fireflies on the lines below. Use *their*, *there*, and *they're* at least once.

_____

_____

_____

_____

_____

_____

Name _____

Beasts & Critters

Read  and Discover

"Silk is a beautiful fabric. Do you know how **it's** made?"

"Silk comes from the silkworm. **Its** cocoon is made of silk fiber."

Circle the boldfaced word that means "it is." Underline the boldfaced word that shows ownership.

Its and *it's* sound the same but are spelled differently and have different meanings. *Its* is a possessive pronoun; it means "belonging to it." *It's* is a contraction that means "it is" or "it has."

See Handbook Section 30

Part 1

Circle the word in parentheses that correctly completes each sentence. (1–15)

Silk fabric is prized for (its/it's) luster. (Its/It's) one of the most luxurious fabrics made.

The silkworm is a kind of caterpillar. Like all caterpillars, the silkworm spins itself into a cocoon during one part of (its/it's) life cycle. (Its/It's) cocoon is made out of one long thread. To make silk, a person gathers a cocoon, unwinds (its/it's) thread, and weaves it with other silk threads.

(Its/It's) well known that mulberry tree leaves are the favorite food of silkworms. The *Bombyx mori* species is the most common source of silk. (Its/It's) diet consists almost entirely of mulberry leaves. (Its/It's) important for silk producers to cultivate healthy mulberry trees. In the first few weeks of (its/it's) life, the silkworm does almost nothing but eat. During those weeks, the silkworm grows to about seventy times (its/it's) original size and increases (its/it's) weight ten thousand times. Most silkworms are cultivated in China. (Its/It's) the biggest producer of raw silk in the world. According to legend, a Chinese empress discovered silk around 2700 B.C. by accidentally dropping a silk cocoon in hot water and unwinding (its/it's) single thread. Because silk was so valuable, the people of China kept (its/it's) origin a secret as long as they were able.

Two thousand years ago, silk became an important product in the Middle East and Europe. Until the third century A.D., only people in China and India knew how to make silk. Finally, four women took the secret to Japan. In A.D. 552, two monks smuggled silkworm eggs and mulberry seeds out of China. (Its/It's) not surprising that other countries soon developed silk industries.

Beasts & Critters

Part 2

Write *its* or *it's* to complete each sentence correctly. Capitalize a word that begins a sentence.

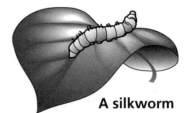

A silkworm

16. Silk cloth is prized for _____ strength and beauty.

17. The silkworm is eaten in some parts of China; _____

    considered a good source of protein.

18. _____ also said to help control high blood pressure.

19. _____ important not to disturb the silkworms while they're building their cocoons.

20. If they are disturbed, _____ possible that they will produce poor threads.

21. Once a silkworm enters _____ cocoon, it takes about two weeks to become a moth.

22. _____ life as a moth is quite short.

23. The moth dies two or three days after laying _____ eggs.

Part 3

Circle the correct word in parentheses to complete each sentence. Then write the answer to each riddle on the lines. Each answer appears in this lesson.

24. (Its/It's) where the silkworm becomes a moth.

    ____ ____ ____ ____ ____ ____

25. (Its/It's) protein makes it a good meal for some.

    ____ ____ ____ ____ ____ ____ ____ ____

26. (Its/It's) the silkworm's favorite food.

    ____ ____ ____ ____ ____ ____ ____ ____   ____ ____ ____ ____ ____ ____

27. (Its/It's) strength, warmth, and beauty make it an ideal material for clothing.

    ____ ____ ____ ____

Name _____

Beasts & Critters

Read  and Discover

I **went**, "What's that loud buzzing noise?"
"It's cicadas calling to each other," **said** Angela.
Shawn **was like**, "Wow!"
Circle the boldfaced word that correctly shows someone is speaking.

Go and *went* mean "move(s) from place to place." *Is like* means "resembles something." Use verbs such as *say*, *ask*, *answer*, *shout*, and *whisper* to indicate that someone is speaking. Avoid using *goes* or *is like* to mean "says." 📣 **Remember to use this information when you speak, too.**

See Handbook Section 29

Part 1 ✏️

Cross out each incorrect usage of *go*, *went*, or *like*. Circle each correct usage of these words. (1–13)

When we went to the park yesterday, we saw thousands of cicadas in the trees.

Shawn went, "Look! They have four wings, and they must be almost two inches long!"

I was like, "Wow! I've never seen a single cicada before, and today they're everywhere I look!"

Angela went, "They've been living underground for seventeen years."

Shawn was like, "Why were they under there for so long?"

Angela went, "That's how long it takes them to grow into adults."

I asked her, "Will they go back to their homes underground?"

Angela was like, "No, they'll fly around for a few weeks, lay eggs, and their lives will be over."

Shawn went, "How sad!"

I was like, "That's their life cycle!"

Angela went, "Yes, their eggs will grow into nymphs that will live underground. Scientists call them *Magicada* because they reappear as if by magic every seventeen years."

I asked, "What other insects are like cicadas?"

Angela said, "I'm not sure. Let's go to the library to find out."

Periodical cicadas live most of their lives underground.

Part 2

Rewrite each sentence to eliminate any incorrect expressions. There is more than one way to rewrite each sentence.

14. I was like, "How do cicadas make that loud buzzing sound?" _____

_____

15. Angela went, "They vibrate special membranes in their abdomens." _____

_____

16. Shawn went, "Why do they do it?" _____

_____

17. Angela goes, "They attract a mate that way." _____

_____

18. Angela was like, "Each species has its own special song." _____

_____

Part 3

Unscramble the letters in parentheses to complete each sentence.

19. "How did you become a cicada expert?" Shawn ___ ___ ___ ___ ___ Angela. (KEDAS)

20. "I read a book about insects," she ___ ___ ___ ___ ___ ___ ___ ___. (WEDENARS)

21. "Oh yuck, a cicada just landed on your arm!" Shawn

___ ___ ___ ___ ___ ___ ___. (TOSUDEH)

22. "Shh, be quiet and maybe we can look at it closely," Angela

___ ___ ___ ___ ___ ___ ___ ___ ___. (SHEPDRIEW)

23. "It has red eyes and red veins on its wings," she ___ ___ ___ ___ quietly. (DASI)

Name _____

Beasts & Critters

Read and Discover

A **good** way to hide from predators is to use a disguise.
Many bugs and insects do this very **well**.
Which boldfaced word tells more about a noun? _____
Which boldfaced word tells more about a verb? _____

Good is an adjective. Use it to describe a noun. *Well* is an adverb. Use it to tell more about a verb. You can also use *well* as an adjective to mean "healthy." **Remember to use this information when you speak, too.**

See Handbook Section 29

Part 1

Circle the correct words in parentheses. (1–13)

Studying insects is a (good/well) hobby for a curious person. I have many (good/well) books about insects. I know these books very (good/well). My favorite book describes the habits of butterflies. Insect camouflage is another topic I know (good/well). Here are a few of the facts I've learned.

Bee

Flower Fly

The flower fly fools predators who mistake it for a bee.

The Kallima butterfly of India has developed a very (good/well) disguise. Its folded wings look like dead leaves, so it stays (good/well) hidden from enemies when it rests on a tree. The walkingstick and the inchworm can also hide themselves (good/well). These insects are (good/well) at blending into wooded areas because they look like twigs.

The viceroy butterfly makes a (good/well) meal for a bird, but eating the monarch butterfly can make a bird sick. Because these butterflies look alike, birds leave them both alone. This trick of mimicking another insect also works (good/well) for the flower fly, which looks like a bee. Predators who know how (good/well) the bee protects itself stay away from both insects.

White or yellow flowers are (good/well) places for crab spiders to hide. These spiders can slowly change color to match the flower they're on. Then predators cannot see them very (good/well).

Part 2 ✏

Read the paragraph below. Then complete items 14–17.

Certain beetles look, taste, smell, and act like certain ants. This protects the beetles from some birds and other predators. Because even the ants cannot tell the difference, the beetles are allowed to live in the ant colonies. The ants even raise the beetle larvae as their own.

14. Write a sentence about these beetles using the word *good*. _____

_____

15. Write a sentence about these beetles using the word *well*. _____

_____

16. Write a sentence about ants using the word *good*. _____

_____

17. Write a sentence about ants using the word *well*. _____

_____

Part 3 ✏

If you were an insect, what kind of disguise would you want? Draw a picture of your ideal insect disguise below. Then write two sentences telling why you think you've created a good disguise for yourself. Use the words *good* and *well* correctly.

18. _____

_____

_____

19. _____

_____

_____

Name _____

Beasts & Critters

Read  and Discover

"We **don't** want to disturb that water strider on the pond."
"It probably **doesn't** even know we're here."
Underline the boldfaced word that is used with a singular subject.
Circle the boldfaced word used with a plural subject.

Use the contraction **doesn't** with singular subjects, including *he*, *she*, and *it*. Use the contraction **don't** with plural subjects, including *we* and *they*. Also use *don't* with *I* and *you*. **Remember to use this information when you speak, too.**

See Handbook Sections 26 and 29

Part 1

Circle the word in parentheses to complete each sentence correctly.

1. Aquatic insects (doesn't/don't) live on land; they live in water.

2. The dragonfly is an aquatic insect, but it (doesn't/don't) live in water for its entire life.

3. The female dragonfly deposits her eggs in the water, but she (doesn't/don't) stay with them.

4. She (doesn't/don't) live more than a few months after laying her eggs.

5. Her eggs develop into nymphs that (doesn't/don't) leave the water for up to five years.

6. Like many other aquatic insects, dragonfly nymphs (doesn't/don't) breathe the way most insects do.

7. They (doesn't/don't) have lungs; they have gills instead.

8. A dragonfly nymph (doesn't/don't) develop wings until it is ready to leave the water.

Dragonflies help people by eating mosquitoes.

9. A dragonfly (doesn't/don't) have legs strong enough to support its large body.

10. Adult dragonflies are among the fastest flying insects, but they (doesn't/don't) walk well.

11. Birds and other predators (doesn't/don't) often catch the swift-flying dragonfly.

12. Although dragonflies appear frightening, they (doesn't/don't) harm people.

13. (Doesn't/Don't) that dragonfly look beautiful?

14. If it lands on you, (doesn't/don't) be afraid.

Beasts & Critters

Part 2

Write *doesn't* or *don't* to complete the sentences correctly. (15–19)

My friend Rhonda and I know a lot about insects. We _____ think many people know more than we do. Her brother _____ know nearly as much as we do.

We know that the name *water bug* _____ refer to just one kind of bug. It refers to five groups of insects that live in water.

Most water bugs feed on other insects, tadpoles, small fish, and salamanders, but the water bug known as the water boatman _____ have the right mouth parts for devouring prey. Instead, it gathers algae and small food particles.

Most water bugs swim, but water striders _____. They walk across the water.

Part 3

Decide whether *doesn't* or *don't* will complete each clue correctly, and cross out the incorrect word. Then use the clues to complete the puzzle. Each answer is found on pages 69–70.

Across

1. They will become dragonflies, but they (doesn't/don't) look like them.
5. They (doesn't/don't) swim.
6. These insects (doesn't/don't) live on land.

Down

2. They (doesn't/don't) often catch dragonflies.
3. They (doesn't/don't) have the right mouth parts for eating insects.
4. It (doesn't/don't) live long after laying its eggs.

Name _____

Beasts & Critters

Read  and Discover

"**Whose** Venus's-flytrap is that?" asked LaShawnna.

"I don't know," Vanessa replied. "**Who's** going to take care of it?"
Underline the boldfaced word that means "who is." Circle the
boldfaced word that shows ownership.

Who's and *whose* sound alike but are spelled differently and have
different meanings. *Who's* is a contraction of "who is" or "who has."
Whose shows ownership or possession.

See Handbook Section 30

Part 1

Circle the correct word in parentheses. (1–10)

I met a girl named Carmen (who's/whose) interested in carnivorous plants. These are plants
(who's/whose) diet includes insects. The plants consume insects because they don't get enough
nitrogen from the soil in which they grow.

(Who's/Whose) seen a plant catch a fly? Anyone (who's/whose) kept a Venus's-flytrap has
probably seen this happen. The Venus's-flytrap is a plant (who's/whose) leaves close like a trap.
An insect unlucky enough to land on the sensitive hairs of the Venus's-flytrap triggers the trap.
The leaves snap shut, and the plant digests the insect. Then the trap opens again.

Pitcher plants are another kind of carnivorous plant. They produce a sweet juice
(who's/whose) smell attracts insects. Insects crawl into a tube-shaped part of the plant and drown
in rainwater that has collected in its watertight "pitcher." The insects can't escape because they
can't climb over the hairs that point downwards inside the tube.

Carmen's father, (who's/whose) an expert on these plants, told me there are some insects that
are able to live inside pitcher plants, (who's/whose) special design destroys so many other creatures. The *Exyra* is one of these. It is a moth (who's/whose) claws are the right size and shape to
grab onto the hairs inside the pitcher plant. Certain mosquito larvae also live inside the pitcher
plant. They swim in the water at the bottom of the tube, (who's/whose) design forms a perfect
aquatic nursery. The mosquito larvae feed on tiny organisms in the water.

Part 2 ✏️

Write *Who's* or *Whose* to complete each question correctly.

11. _____ a budding expert on carnivorous plants?

12. _____ leaves snap shut to trap insects?

13. _____ seen giant carnivorous plants in movies?

14. _____ trying to grow carnivorous plants in her garden?

15. _____ camera may I borrow to take a picture?

A Venus's-flytrap

Part 3 ✏️

Write a question to go with each answer below. Use *who's* or *whose* in each question you write.

16. My cousin Ariel is an expert on carnivorous plants.

    _____

    _____

17. That magnifying glass is Ariel's.

    _____

    _____

18. The red raincoat belongs to me.

    _____

    _____

19. The man with the flyswatter is my uncle Orestes.

    _____

    _____

Name _____

Beasts & Critters

Read and Discover

Look at those **two** ants. Are they on their way **to** our picnic basket? If we don't move it now, it will be **too** late!

Which boldfaced word means "in the direction of"? _____

Which boldfaced word names a number? _____

Which boldfaced word means "very"? _____

The words *to, too,* and *two* sound the same but have different meanings and spellings. *To* can be a preposition that means "in the direction of." *To* can also be used with a verb to form an *infinitive*, as in the sentence *We like to watch ants. Too* is an adverb and means "also" or "very." *Two* means the number 2.

See Handbook Section 30

Part 1

Circle the word in parentheses that correctly completes each sentence. (1–12)

There are many kinds of ants, each with its own way of gathering food. (To/Too/Two) kinds that fascinate me are army ants and leaf-cutter ants. Dairying ants are interesting, (to/too/two).

Army ants hunt other insects and spiders for food. They sometimes kill larger animals, (to/too/two). Army ant colonies can have up (to/too/two) several million members. They march in narrow columns across the land or through underground tunnels. The ants work as a group (to/too/two) bite and kill their prey. Some species alternate between periods of hunting and periods of rest. Each period may last for (to/too/two) or more weeks.

Leaf-cutter ants work hard for their food, (to/too/two), but they don't hunt other animals. Leaf-cutter ants are farmers. These ants use their powerful jaws (to/too/two) cut pieces of leaves from plants. They carry the leaves (to/too/two) their underground nests, where other workers chew the leaves into a soft paste. The ants grow their food, a kind of fungus, on the leaf paste. Tens of thousands of ants live in one leaf-cutter colony, and each has a job (to/too/two) do.

Dairying ants are similar (to/too/two) human farmers. They eat a liquid called *honeydew* that is produced by aphids. When the ants stroke the aphids with their antennae, the aphids produce drops of honeydew. The process is similar (to/too/two) the way dairy farmers milk cows.

Part 2 ✏

Write *to, too,* or *two* to complete each sentence correctly.

13. "Let's go _____ the park," Anika suggested.

14. "No, there are _____ many ants in the park," Olivia replied.

15. "We could watch the ants _____ see what they do," said Anika.

16. "But there are only _____ of us, and millions of them!" objected Olivia.

17. "I don't think we'll be in _____ much danger," Anika reassured her.

18. "In this part of the country there aren't _____ many ants that bite humans."

19. "Besides, they won't pay any attention _____ us unless we disturb them," she said.

20. "Let's go and see if we can find at least _____ different kinds of ants."

21. "Well, I suppose the _____ of us can handle that," Olivia finally agreed.

22. "Let's bring this book about ants _____ the park with us," Anika suggested.

Part 3 ✏

Complete the poem by writing *to, too,* and *two.* (23–25)

The ants march past us, two by _____.

What do you think they're going _____ do?

Nothing stops them. They march right through.

Mud and sand and tall grass, _____.

Now the leaders give a sign.

Word is passed back through the line,

"Cake ahead! Take a bite!

But stay in line and be polite!"

Name _____

Beasts & Critters

Read  and Discover

"**Leave** me alone. I don't want to help you **raise** money to save endangered insects."

"But you promised you would **let** me have five dollars. The numbers of endangered animals will **rise** if you don't help."

Which boldfaced word means "allow"? _____

Which boldfaced word means "go away from"? _____

Which boldfaced word means "collect"? _____

Which boldfaced word means "go up"? _____

 The verbs *leave* and *let* are often confused. *Leave* means "to let remain in a place" or "to go away from." *Let* means "to allow." The verbs *rise* and *raise* are also often confused. *Rise* does not need a direct object. *Raise* must be followed by a direct object. **Remember to use this information when you speak, too.**

See Handbook Section 29

Part 1

Circle the correct word in parentheses. (1–12)

"You won't believe what I saw when I (rose/raised) my binoculars!" Donna exclaimed.

"What is it? (Leave/Let) me see!" Kavika demanded.

"It's a weta, one of the world's largest insects!" said Donna. "They grow to four inches long."

"(Leave/Let) me ask you something," said Kavika. "Are wetas becoming endangered?"

"That's true," said Donna. "The number of wetas is dropping because the number of people moving onto the land where they live is (rising/raising). Wetas live in New Zealand."

"Is there anything we can do to help the weta population (rise/raise)?" Kavika wondered.

"Look," Donna interrupted. "Now the weta is (rising/raising) its hind legs and kicking at a rat! The rat might (leave/let) the weta escape."

"Maybe we should (leave/let) now, before we frighten the weta ourselves," Kavika suggested.

"Good idea," Donna said. "Tomorrow let's try to come back just as the sun (rises/raises)."

"I can (leave/let) my home before dawn," Kavika said. "I hope the park ranger will (leave/let) us enter the park that early. I don't know whether she'll be here to (rise/raise) the entrance gate."

Beasts & Critters

Part 2 ✏️

Complete each sentence with your own words. Use *leave, let, rise,* or *raise* correctly.

13. Let me help you _____

_____

14. If I raise _____

_____

15. Every day, we rise _____

_____

16. If we leave _____

_____

17. If my father lets _____

_____

Part 3 ✏️

Use forms of *leave, let, rise,* and *raise* to complete this puzzle.

Across
  2. ___ me show you my photographs of giant insects.
  3. You must ___ the library by 6 p.m.
  4. The sun always ___ in the east.

Down
  1. I ___ the flag yesterday.
  2. Ramón always ___ me use his binoculars.
  4. Does anyone ___ wetas for a living?

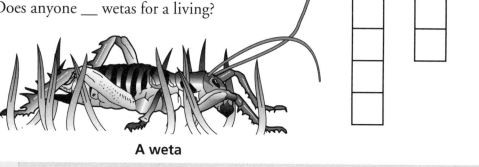

A weta

Name _____

Beasts & Critters

Read  and Discover

"I **swim** almost every day. I **swam** in a pond yesterday and saw a spider in the water! I have never **swimmed** away from anything so fast!" Cross out the boldfaced word that is used incorrectly.

The verbs *fly*, *run*, and *swim* are **irregular**. They do not add *-ed* in the past tense. 📣 **Remember this information when you speak, too.**

Present	Past	With *have, has,* or *had*
fly/flies	flew	flown
run/runs	ran	run
swim/swims	swam	swum

See Handbook Section 17

Part 1

Circle the correct word in parentheses.

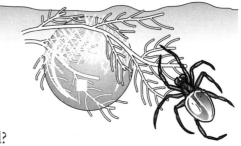

Water spiders trap air in underwater nests and use this air to breathe.

1. Have you ever seen a spider (run/ran)?

2. Has a spider ever (flied/flown) past you out at sea?

3. Has a spider ever (swimmed/swum) by you in a pond?

4. Once I watched a wolf spider (run/ran) to capture its prey.

5. The ant had (ran/run) quickly, but it was no match for the spider.

6. I have been watching that fisher spider for an hour, but it hasn't (swam/swum) yet.

7. Fisher spiders can (swim/swam) well.

8. That water spider lives underwater; it (swimmed/swam) fast to catch its morning meal.

9. Before we had even begun to eat, a grass spider had (ran/run) across our picnic blanket.

10. The jumping spider pounced on its prey from several inches away. It couldn't have moved any faster if it had (flew/flown).

11. The female black widow spider is poisonous. I (runned/ran) away the first time I saw one!

12. A mosquito (flyed/flew) straight into the labyrinth spider's web.

13. I saw a water spider's nest as I (swam/swum) across the pond.

14. I had (swam/swum) in that pond many times without ever having seen one before.

Beasts & Critters

Part 2

Imagine that you have discovered a new species of giant spider that can fly, run, and swim. Write about this unusual creature. Use present- and past-tense forms of the verbs in the word bank. Don't forget to use *have, has,* or *had* when you need to.

fly	run	swim

15. _____

_____

16. _____

_____

17. _____

_____

18. _____

_____

Part 3

Use forms of *fly, run,* and *swim* to complete this crossword puzzle.

Across

2. Long before dinosaurs lived, ancestors of insects had __ in the oceans.
3. Dragonflies with over two-foot wingspans __ around dinosaurs' heads.
4. Prehistoric sea scorpions __ swiftly and grew up to eight feet long.

Down

1. If I saw a prehistoric insect coming, I would __ away.
2. People __ in the sea today without worrying about scorpions.
3. Imagine the creatures that have __ over these lands.

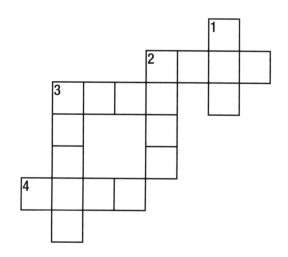

Name _____

Beasts & Critters

Proofreading Others' Writing

Read this report about insect pests and find the mistakes. Use the proofreading marks below to show how each mistake should be corrected.

Proofreading Marks

Mark	Means	Example
∧	add	Insects are the most numerous creatures ^on Earth.
℘	take away	Insects are the the most numerous creatures on Earth.
≡	make into a capital letter	insects are the most numerous creatures on Earth.
⊙	add a period	Insects are the most numerous creatures on Earth⊙
/	make into a lowercase letter	Insects are the most Numerous creatures on Earth.
(sp)	fix spelling	Insects are the most numerous creachures on Earth.

Insect Pests

Your probably familiar with a number of insect pests, such as mosquitoes and cockroaches. These to insects are annoying and can carry diseases. Their are agricultural pests that cause more damage and hardship. Did you know that insects destroy almost 37 percent of the crops grown in the united States yearly? The cost of the damage, plus the cost of controlling pests, is $7 billion a year. Whose paying for this? You pay some of this the cost when you buy you're groceries.

Its amazing to think that all this damage is done by only a few hundred of the thousands of insect spesies in the United states. Most harmful insects damage particular types of plants. The boll weevil destroys the cotton plant. The young gypsy Moth kills trees The japanese beetle damages the leaves and fruit of plants. The corn borer prevents corn plants from growing good.

They're are a number of ways too control insect pests. Spraying insecticides on crops is one of the most effective. Unfortunately, insecticides doesn't kill only the bad insects. They can also harm helpful insects. When I heard that, I was like, "I don't think using large quantities is a good idea." Now I'm trying to rise awareness of safe alternatives.

Proofreading Your Own Writing

You can use the list below to help you find and fix mistakes in your own writing. Write the titles of your own stories or reports in the blanks on top of the chart. Then use the questions to check your work. Make a check mark (✓) in each box after you have checked that item.

Titles

Proofreading Checklist for Unit 3

Have I used these words correctly: *your* and *you're; its* and *it's; their, there,* and *they're; who's* and *whose; to, too,* and *two*?				
Have I avoided using *go, went, is like,* and *was like* incorrectly?				
Have I used *good, well, doesn't, don't, leave, let, rise,* and *raise* correctly?				
Have I used past-tense forms of irregular verbs correctly?				

Also Remember . . .

Does each sentence begin with a capital letter?				
Does each sentence end with the right mark?				
Have I spelled each word correctly?				
Have I used commas correctly?				

Your Own List
Use this space to write your own list of things to check in your writing.

Name

Beasts & Critters

Usage

Circle the word in parentheses that correctly completes each sentence.

1. "Is that (your/you're) book about insects, Mikhail?" asked Talia.

2. "Yes, I was just reading about butterflies and (their/there/they're) migrating habits," Mikhail answered.

3. "Did you learn about the butterfly's life cycle, (to/too/two)?" Talia asked.

4. "Yes. The butterfly begins life as a caterpillar (who's/whose) main activity is eating," Mikhail explained.

5. "Caterpillars store most of (their/there/they're) food to use as energy later," he added.

6. "After at least (to/too/two) weeks, caterpillars are ready to become butterflies," he said.

7. "A caterpillar (who's/whose) ready to do this forms a hard shell around itself," said Mikhail.

8. "(Its/It's) shell is called a *chrysalis*, and this stage of a butterfly's life is called the *pupal stage*," he said.

9. "The pupa can stay inside the chrysalis for a few days or for more than a year. (Its/It's) different for each species of butterfly," Mikhail said.

10. "What does the pupa do in (their/there/they're)?" asked Talia.

11. "The pupa changes into a butterfly inside (its/it's) chrysalis," Mikhail explained.

12. "That's all I know about the butterfly's life cycle," he said. "(Your/You're) going to have to read the book yourself if you want to learn more."

Circle the errors. Write *C* after each sentence that is written correctly.

13. Victoria was like, "What kind of insect is that?" ___

14. I go, "It's a ladybug, a kind of beetle." ___

15. She said, "I like the way it looks with those black dots on its red wings." ___

Beasts & Critters

81

G.U.M.

More Usage

Choose the correct word in parentheses to complete the sentences. Then write the word in the blank.

16. My cousin gave me _____ advice about camping. (good/well)

17. She said, "You'll be sorry if you _____ bring insect repellent." (doesn't/don't)

18. Mosquitoes will _____ your campsite if you light citronella candles. (leave/let)

19. When the moon _____, mosquitoes become less active. (rises/raises)

20. This liquid insect repellent also works _____. (good/well)

21. Last summer, I had to _____ the mountains after just two days because the mosquitoes bothered me so much. (leave/let)

22. I'm thinking about staying home from the family camping trip this year, but I'm afraid to _____ the issue with my parents. (rise/raise)

23. They never _____ me stay home by myself. (leave/let)

24. It _____ even seem worthwhile to ask them. (doesn't/don't)

Circle the correct form of the verb in parentheses.

25. Last night a moth (flied/flew) right into my bedroom.

26. I (ran/runned) over to the window to look for more flying insects.

27. A different moth had (flew/flown) into my bedroom the night before.

28. I became interested in insects last summer when I (swimmed/swam) in a pond and noticed how many different kinds of creatures lived there.

29. I had (swam/swum) for hours when I finally stopped for lunch.

30. Before the end of that day I had (ran/run) to the library twice for books about aquatic insects.

Name _____

Beasts & Critters

FAMILY LEARNING OPPORTUNITIES

In Unit 3 of *G.U.M.* we are learning how to use words that can be confusing, such as *its* and *it's* and *their*, *there*, and *they're*. The activities on these pages give extra practice with some of the concepts we're learning. You can help reinforce the information your child is learning in school by choosing one or more activities to complete at home.

He Said, She Said (Being Careful with *Go* and *Like*)

Invite your child to relate a conversation he or she recently had with one of his or her friends. Ask your child to speak for at least 60 seconds. Notice whether your child uses *go, went, is like,* or *was like* in place of *say* or another verb. Each time this happens, have your child begin his or her report of the conversation again from the beginning. Then switch roles. See who can complete his or her entire explanation in the fewest attempts.

Example	Incorrect: "Caroline was like, 'I can't believe it!' Then I went, 'It's true.'"
	Correct: "Caroline said, 'I can't believe it!' Then I replied, 'It's true.'"

Guessing Game (*Its* and *It's*)

Have your child think of an insect or other kind of bug that is familiar to both of you. Then have your child write three or four sentences describing the creature using *its* and *it's*. Ask your child not to tell you the name of the insect or bug. Then read the sentences and try to guess what creature your child has described.

Example	**Its** sting can be painful. **It's** a hard worker. **Its** body has yellow and black stripes.

Word Search (*Your* and *You're*; *Doesn't* and *Don't*; *Who's* and *Whose*; *To, Too, Two*)

There are nine words hidden in the puzzle. Some of them are missing apostrophes. Work with your child to find all nine. Then ask your child to write each word correctly in a sentence.

W	H	O	S	E	I	L	T	D	A
Y	R	U	L	M	B	K	W	O	I
O	T	B	W	C	T	O	O	N	H
U	O	C	H	F	D	I	L	T	U
R	I	Y	O	U	R	Q	V	C	L
E	X	Z	S	D	O	E	S	N	T

Crossword Puzzle (Irregular Verbs: *Fly, Run, Swim*; *Leave* and *Let*; *Rise* and *Raise*)

Work with your child to complete this puzzle. Each answer is a form of *fly, run, swim, leave, let, rise,* or *raise.*

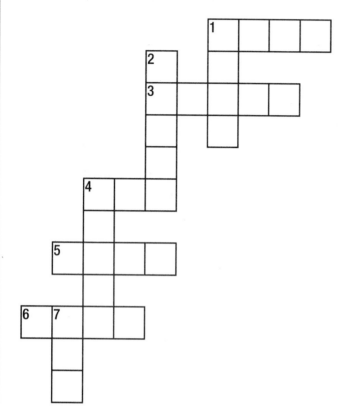

Across

1. Charlene has __ more than anyone else at the pool.
3. I have to __ at 3:00 p.m.
4. We __ to catch the bus this morning.
5. Let's sit outside and watch the moon __.
6. A dragonfly __ towards me at top speed this morning.

Down

1. Yesterday Jeff __ across the lake for the first time.
2. I have never __ in an airplane.
4. My aunt and uncle __ dairy cows on their farm.
7. Will you __ me ride your bicycle?

Poetry in Motion (*Their, There, They're*)

Encourage your child to write a short poem about insects. Ask him or her to begin one line with *their,* one line with *there,* and one line with *they're.*

My Favorite (*Good* and *Well*)

Invite your child to write a paragraph about something he or she does well. Have your child use the words *good* and *well* correctly. Then encourage your child to draw a picture showing himself or herself doing the activity he or she described in the paragraph.

Example

Jumping rope is my favorite activity. I am particularly **good** at double dutch. When I first started, I couldn't turn the ropes very **well**. Now I am very **good** at it. I can also jump faster than anyone else on my block.

Name _____

Beasts & Critters

Read  and Discover

a. Few athletes can excel at several different sports events.

b. **They** usually concentrate on one or two of **them**.

Which boldfaced word replaces the word *athletes*? _____

Which boldfaced word replaces the phrase *several different sports events*? _____

Which word is the subject of sentence b.? _____

A pronoun can take the place of a subject or an object in a sentence. **Subject pronouns** include *I, he, she, we,* and *they.* (Subject pronouns are said to be in the subjective *case.*) **Object pronouns** can be used after an action verb or a preposition. Object pronouns include *me, him, her, us,* and *them.* (Object pronouns are said to be in the objective *case.*) The pronouns *it* and *you* can be either subjects or objects. ◀ **Remember to use this information when you speak, too.**

See Handbook Section 16

Part 1

Circle each boldfaced word that is a subject pronoun. Underline each boldfaced word that is an object pronoun.

1. My uncle told **me** about Babe Didrikson Zaharias, the famous athlete.

2. **He** thinks Babe is the greatest woman athlete of all time.

3. **He** is impressed that **she** played so many different sports.

4. Babe tried basketball, baseball, golf, tennis, swimming, track and field, and figure skating; **she** excelled at all of **them**.

5. **She** won two gold medals at the 1932 Olympic Games.

6. **They** were for the javelin throw and the 80-meter hurdles.

7. Babe won a silver medal at the same competition. **It** was for the high jump.

8. At a track meet earlier that year, **she** had set four world records in three hours.

9. When Babe took up golf, **she** won 17 tournaments in a row.

10. A trophy for outstanding female athletes was named after **her**.

11. My uncle and **I** have decided to read more about **her**.

12. **We** think her life story can teach **us** a lot about courage and perseverance.

Babe Zaharias was one of the most famous women athletes of all time.

Unforgettable Folks

Part 2

Rewrite each sentence. Replace each boldfaced phrase with a subject pronoun or an object pronoun.

13. **The Associated Press** named **Babe Didrikson Zaharias** "Woman Athlete of the Year" six times between 1932 and 1954. _____

_____

14. **Babe** concentrated on playing golf then. _____

_____

15. **Many new golf fans** came to watch **Babe** play in golf tournaments. _____

_____

16. Sadly, **Babe** was diagnosed with cancer in 1953. _____

_____

17. But **cancer** couldn't keep **Babe** from doing what **Babe** loved. _____

_____

18. **Sports fans** were amazed to see **Babe** win **the U.S. Women's Open golf tournament** in 1954. _____

_____

Part 3

Write two or three sentences about playing your favorite sport. Use subject and object pronouns in your sentences.

_____

_____

_____

Name _____

Unforgettable Folks

Read  and Discover

   a. Julia and **me** read about astronaut Ellen Ochoa.
   b. Mrs. Gomez told Julia and **me** about her work at NASA.
If you delete "Julia and" from each sentence, which sentence sounds correct? ____

> Use a **subject pronoun** in a compound subject. Use an **object pronoun** in a compound direct object, compound indirect object, or compound object of a preposition. If you are unsure which pronoun form to use, say the sentence to yourself without the other part of the compound. For example, *Julia and me read about astronaut Ellen Ochoa* becomes *Me read about astronaut Ellen Ochoa.* You can hear that *me* should be replaced with *I.*
> 📢 **Remember to use this information when you speak, too.**
>
> **See Handbook** Sections 16 and 29

Part 1 ✏️

Circle the correct pronoun in each pair. Write *S* if you chose a subject pronoun and *O* if you chose an object pronoun.

1. Mrs. Gomez took Mario, Pedro, Julia, and (I/me) to hear Ellen Ochoa speak. ____

2. Pedro and (I/me) already knew who Ellen Ochoa was. ____

3. (He/Him) and Mario asked us how she became a famous astronaut. ____

4. We explained to Mario and (he/him) that in 1990 Ochoa became the first Latina astronaut to work for the National Aeronautics and Space Administration (NASA). ____

5. Mrs. Gomez reminded Julia and (I/me) that she was one of only 23 graduates from NASA's 1990 astronaut class. ____

6. I felt as if Ochoa was speaking directly to Mrs. Gomez and (we/us). ____

7. After the lecture, we went to the front of the room to meet (she/her). ____

8. Ochoa shook hands with Mario and (she/her). ____

9. She told us about the training (she/her) and the other astronauts had completed. ____

10. But it paid off in 1993 when (she/her) and another astronaut orbited Earth. ____

11. (He/Him) and Ochoa measured the temperature and chemical levels in the atmosphere. ____

12. I nodded when Ochoa told Julia and (I/me) to continue studying math and science. ____

Part 2

Rewrite the sentences. Substitute a pronoun for each boldfaced noun.

13. **Pedro** and **Julia** went to Florida to see the space shuttle launch. _____

_____

14. A tour guide directed Pedro and **Julia** to the launching pad. _____

_____

15. **Mario** and Carla watched on TV as the space shuttle took off. _____

_____

16. Julia told **Carla** and Mario that the shuttle would orbit Earth. _____

_____

17. Carla told **Julia** and **Pedro** that she wants to be an astronaut one day. _____

_____

Part 3

Draw a line to connect each sentence with the pronoun pair that could replace the boldfaced nouns in that sentence. Circle pronouns that should be capitalized.

Jed and **Leticia** have been inside a space shuttle.	her and him
Sharon and **Steve** didn't believe them.	him and her
Jed told **Sharon** and **Steve** that it was in a museum.	she and he
Sharon asked **Jed** and **Leticia** if she could come next time.	he and she

Name _____

Unforgettable Folks

Read and Discover

Mohandas K. Gandhi was a great spiritual and political leader of India. **He** led India to independence.

Circle the phrase the boldfaced pronoun replaces. Draw an arrow from the pronoun to the circled phrase.

> An **antecedent** is the word or phrase a pronoun refers to. The antecedent includes a noun. When you write a pronoun, be sure its antecedent is clear. Pronouns must also **agree** with their antecedents. An antecedent and pronoun agree when they have the same number (singular or plural), case (subjective or objective), and gender (male or female).

See Handbook Section 16

Part 1

Circle the antecedent of each boldfaced pronoun.

1. Mohandas Gandhi was born in India in 1869. In 1891, **he** became a lawyer and moved to South Africa.

2. White South Africans discriminated against native people. **They** also discriminated against immigrants.

3. This racial discrimination made Gandhi angry. He responded to **it** by leading a movement for Indian rights in South Africa.

***Satyagraha*, the name of Gandhi's protest method, means "steadfastness in truth."**

4. Gandhi developed a method of opposing injustice. **It** was based on the principles of courage, nonviolence, and truth.

5. People who follow his method refuse to fight, even when others are attacking **them**.

6. In this way, nonviolent protestors show how strongly they believe in **their** ideals.

7. In 1915 Gandhi returned to India. At that time, **it** was part of the British Empire.

8. The British were in charge of the government and most businesses. In general, Indian people were not treated as equals by **them**.

9. Gandhi was the leader of a movement to return power to Indians. He devoted his life to **it**.

10. Nonviolence was a dangerous form of protest. Gandhi was jailed for **his** beliefs many times.

11. Gandhi devoted himself to the struggle for independence. He fasted to draw attention to **it**.

Part 2

Write the pronoun that could replace or relate to each boldfaced word or phrase. Capitalize a word that begins a sentence.

12. **People all over India** began to follow Gandhi's movement. _____ joined in protesting British injustices.

13. Gandhi taught **his followers** to be fair to people of all races and religions. It sometimes was hard for _____ to overcome their prejudices.

14. **People** began to call Gandhi *Mahatma,* which means "Great Soul." This showed _____ respect for him.

15. **India** finally won _____ independence from Britain in 1947.

16. Indian Muslims decided to create **their own separate nation.** _____ is called *Pakistan.*

17. **Gandhi** was disappointed that Hindus and Muslims could not live together in peace. _____ tried to stop them from dividing India into two countries.

18. Sadly, **a man who was a Hindu fanatic** killed Gandhi in 1948. _____ disagreed with Gandhi's wish that Muslims and Hindus live together.

Part 3

Circle the pronoun in each clue. Then find the four antecedents in the puzzle. All the antecedents appear in this lesson.

19. Gandhi worked for it in India.

20. They wanted a separate nation.

21. It was a British colony.

22. He followed the principles of courage, nonviolence, and truth.

I	N	D	E	P	E	N	D	E	N	C	E
T	A	O	P	F	Q	S	V	Y	G	B	E
X	P	X	P	R	I	R	Z	Z	A	R	O
B	G	I	E	H	N	P	G	Q	N	L	O
L	P	D	T	J	D	N	R	K	D	W	X
I	M	U	S	L	I	M	S	A	H	O	Q
U	T	F	J	C	A	G	M	Z	I	L	P

Name _____

Unforgettable Folks

Read and Discover

Sitting Bull was a Sioux chief **who** became famous for his wisdom and bravery. _____

He was dedicated to protecting the homeland of his people, for **whom** the coming of land-hungry settlers was a disaster. _____

Underline the clauses that include *who* or *whom*. After each sentence, write whether *who* or *whom* is a subject or an object.

Use **who** as the **subject** of a sentence or a clause. Use **whom** as the **object** of a verb or a preposition. Remember to use this information when you speak, too.

See Handbook Sections 16 and 29

Part 1

Circle a word in parentheses to complete each sentence correctly.

1. Sitting Bull was a member of the Hunkpapa Sioux people, (who/whom) had lived in present-day South Dakota for many generations.

2. His parents, (who/whom) saw that he was a careful child, called him *Hunk-es-ni*.

3. The Crow people (who/whom) lived nearby were long-standing enemies of the Sioux.

4. The Crow people (who/whom) *Hunk-es-ni* fought did not think the boy's name fit him.

5. The young man proved himself a brave warrior and earned the name of his father, (who/whom) had been called Sitting Bull.

6. As land-hungry settlers moved west, they took land from the Sioux, (who/whom) had lived there for a very long time.

7. Sitting Bull grew into a brave and wise man (who/whom) the Hunkpapas chose to be chief.

8. In 1866, Sitting Bull led an attack on the U.S. soldiers (who/whom) had been occupying Sioux territory.

9. The U.S. government sent officials (who/whom) wanted Sitting Bull and his people to move to a reservation.

10. He led his people to Canada instead of agreeing to the demands of men for (who/whom) he had little respect.

Part 2 ✏️

Complete a question for each answer.

11. Sitting Bull was a Hunkpapa Sioux chief.

Who _____

_____ ?

**Sitting Bull led his
people to Canada.**

12. Sitting Bull led his people against land-hungry settlers.

Against whom _____ ?

13. He defeated General Custer in a battle known as "Custer's Last Stand."

_____ whom?

14. Government officials wanted the Sioux people to live on a reservation.

Who _____ ?

15. Settlers wanted to live on land that the Sioux had long occupied.

Who _____ ?

Part 3 ✏️

Imagine that you are able to interview Sitting Bull. Write three questions you would ask him.
Use *who* or *whom* in each question.

16. _____

_____

17. _____

_____

18. _____

_____

Name _____

Unforgettable Folks

Read and Discover

Students of United States **history** learn about Harriet Tubman's heroic actions.

Circle the boldfaced noun above that is the simple subject. Is the noun singular or plural? _____ Underline the verb.

> The **subject** and its **verb must agree**. Add *s* or *es* to a regular verb in the present tense when the subject is a singular noun or *he, she,* or *it*. Do not add *s* or *es* to a regular verb in the present tense when the subject is a plural noun or *I, you, we,* or *they*. Be sure that the verb agrees with its subject and not with the object of a preposition that comes before the verb. **Remember to use this information when you speak, too.**

See Handbook Section 17

Part 1

Circle the simple subject in each sentence. Then underline the correct form of each verb in parentheses.

1. Many people across the United States (admire/admires) Harriet Tubman's courage.

2. Her heroic efforts against slavery (is/are) well known.

3. Tubman's daring escape from slavery in 1849 (show/shows) her strong desire for freedom.

4. The risks she took to help others find freedom (reveal/reveals) her compassion.

5. Monuments marking buildings on the Underground Railroad, an escape route, (remind/reminds) us of the danger she faced.

6. The route taken by those fleeing slavery (stretch/stretches) north through New York, Pennsylvania, and Canada.

Harriet Tubman helped about 300 people flee to freedom.

7. People who visit these places (learn/learns) about the hundreds of families who helped enslaved African Americans escape to freedom.

8. Most people (agree/agrees) that these families were also heroes.

9. At one Wisconsin site, a hand-dug tunnel (lead/leads) to another building.

10. An emergency exit such as this (allow/allows) a person to escape quickly.

11. Many people (call/calls) Tubman "the conductor" because she helped people escape on the Underground Railroad.

Unforgettable Folks

Part 2

Write a verb to complete each sentence. Use words from the word bank if you like.

teach teaches	admire admires	tell tells	include includes

12. Some descendants of enslaved African Americans _____ family
     stories about the Underground Railroad.

13. These stories about the Underground Railroad _____ us about a
     difficult time in U.S. history.

14. This poster of people who opposed slavery _____ Frederick
     Douglass and Sojourner Truth.

15. Today, Americans of all backgrounds _____ these heroic people.

Part 3

Use the clues to complete the puzzle. Each answer appears somewhere in this lesson.

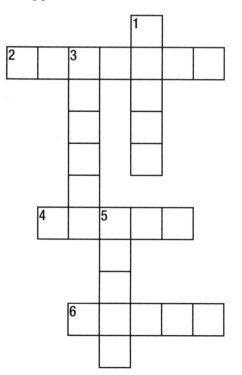

Across
2. Mr. Abrams __ United States history.
4. Students in his class __ about Harriet Tubman.
6. Mr. Abrams __ them stories about the Underground Railroad.

Down
1. This map __ the route people followed when they escaped from slavery.
3. I __ their courage.
5. Most people __ that Harriet Tubman is a true hero.

Name _____

Unforgettable Folks

Read and Discover

a. Brazilians **are** proud of their heroic ancestor, Zumbi.

b. Zumbi **is** admired by Brazilians of all backgrounds who believe in racial equality.

Which sentence has a singular subject? ___ Circle the boldfaced verb in that sentence.

Which sentence has a plural subject? ___ Underline the boldfaced verb in that sentence.

Am, is, was, are, and **were** are forms of the verb *be*. Use *am* after the pronoun *I*. Use *is* or *was* after a singular subject or after the pronoun *he, she,* or *it*. Use *are* or *were* after a plural subject or after the pronoun *we, you,* or *they.* **Remember to use this information when you speak, too.**

See Handbook Sections 17 and 29

Part 1

Underline the correct form of *be* in each sentence.

1. In the sixteenth century, many African people (was/were) captured and brought to Brazil by Portuguese colonists.

2. They wanted freedom and (was/were) determined to escape.

3. Some of them (was/were) able to run away and create their own communities in northeastern Brazil.

Brazil is the largest country in South America.

4. Zumbi (was/were) born in one of these communities, Palmares, in 1655.

5. As a baby, Zumbi (was/were) captured in an attack and given to a priest in a faraway city.

6. When he (was/were) fifteen, he escaped and returned to Palmares.

7. Later, he (was/were) chosen as king and military leader of the settlement.

8. Under his rule, the people of Palmares (was/were) able to survive Portuguese attacks.

9. The government feared that Palmares (was/were) an example for enslaved people.

10. Eventually, the outpost of freedom (was/were) destroyed and Zumbi was killed.

11. In 1978 the anniversary of his death (was/were) commemorated with a holiday, Zumbi Day.

12. Today, the holiday (is/are) called National Black Consciousness Day.

Unforgettable Folks

Part 2

Write a form of the verb *be* to complete each sentence correctly. (13–19)

Where _____ you during last year's Carnival celebration? I _____

visiting relatives in Brazil. We _____ part of a parade honoring the Afro-Brazilian

hero Zumbi. I _____ so happy I could go to the festival. I hope you

_____ able to visit Brazil one day. Brazil _____ a fascinating place. I

_____ returning there next year.

Part 3

Imagine that you and a friend travel backward in time and visit Palmares. Write four sentences describing the things you see and the people you meet. Use a form of the verb *be* in each sentence.

20. _____

_____

21. _____

_____

22. _____

_____

23. _____

_____

Name _____

Unforgettable Folks

Read and Discover

In 247 B.C. Hannibal **was born** in Carthage, a city in North Africa. At that time Carthage and Rome **were trying** to gain control of the Mediterranean region. These cities **are fighting** three major wars between 264 and 146 B.C.

Circle the boldfaced verb phrase that does not give a correct sense of time.

All words in a sentence must work together to give an accurate sense of time. Make sure each **verb** is in the **proper tense** for the time period being discussed. ◀️📢 **Remember to use this information when you speak, too.**

See Handbook Section 17

Part 1

Underline the verb or verb phrase that gives the correct sense of time.

1. Hannibal (was/has been) Carthage's greatest military and political leader.

2. Rome's powerful legions had conquered many lands, and the people of Carthage (fear/feared) their land might be next.

3. In 219 B.C. Hannibal (attacked/has attacked) Saguntum, a city in Spain that was friendly to the Romans.

4. He (mounted/was mounting) a campaign to surprise Rome with an attack from the North.

5. This was a daring plan because the Alps (are protecting/protect) northern Italy.

6. Hannibal (assembled/assembles) a force of 60,000 soldiers, horses, and even elephants.

7. In those days elephants (were used/are used) like tanks to break through enemy lines.

8. Many of Hannibal's soldiers (were killed/are killed) by the cold or by mountain tribes.

9. Nevertheless, Hannibal and 26,000 of his soldiers (reached/will reach) the Po Valley.

10. Although he was outnumbered, Hannibal (won/wins) many battles against the Romans.

11. At the Battle of Cannae the Romans (suffered/will suffer) their worst defeat ever.

12. Although Rome won the war in the end, Hannibal (is remembered/had been remembered) as one of the greatest military leaders of all time.

Unforgettable Folks

Part 2

Rewrite the following sentences to indicate that the events took place in the past.

13. Publius Cornelius Scipio, a Roman general, begins to win battles against the

    Carthaginians in Spain and Africa. _____

    _____

14. Hannibal is called home to Carthage to fight him. _____

    _____

15. Scipio finally defeats Hannibal in 202 B.C. and imprisons the great general. _____

    _____

16. Hannibal escapes and returns home to Carthage. _____

    _____

17. Hannibal eventually becomes the ruler of Carthage. _____

    _____

Part 3

Write two sentences using the characters and verbs in the word bank. Use a different verb tense in each sentence. Check to make sure the verb tenses are correct.

Characters	Action verb	Tense/time
Hannibal	lead	Past
Scipio	defeat	Present
Carthaginian Army	follow	Future

18. _____

    _____

19. _____

    _____

Name _____

Unforgettable Folks

Read and Discover

a. Firefighters and police officers are everyday heroes.
b. A firefighter or a police officer often risks death in order to help others.

Circle the compound subject in each sentence. Underline the verb in each sentence. Which sentence has a verb that goes with a singular subject? ____

A **compound subject** and its **verb** must agree. If a compound subject includes the conjunction *and*, it is plural and needs a plural verb. If a compound subject includes *or* or *nor*, the verb must agree with the last item in the subject. **Remember to use this information when you speak, too.**

See Handbook Sections 10 and 17

Part 1

Look at the compound subject in each sentence. Circle the conjunction. Then underline the correct verb.

1. Every day many men and women (perform/performs) acts of heroism.

2. After an engineer or a construction worker (dangle/dangles) in midair to repair a bridge, everyone can travel more safely.

3. When a police officer or a firefighter (respond/responds), he or she acts courageously.

4. Whether a house or a forest (is/are) burning, firefighters rush to extinguish the flames.

5. Doctors and scientists (race/races) to find cures and treatments for diseases.

6. Sometimes a scientist or a researcher (spend/spends) decades searching for a vaccine.

7. Paramedics and rescue workers (rush/rushes) to the scene of an accident.

8. Rescue dogs and their owners (travel/travels) great distances to help find earthquake survivors.

9. When war or natural disaster (strike/strikes), Red Cross workers bring food and medicine.

10. Red Cross workers and volunteers (provide/provides) supplies to people.

11. Each time a bus driver or a train conductor (assist/assists) a disabled person, he or she makes transportation more accessible.

Unforgettable Folks

Part 2

Rewrite these sentences to correct the errors.

12. Sometimes a seal or a dolphin wash up on the beach. _____

_____

13. A worker or a volunteer at the Marine Mammal Center return the stranded animal to the

water. _____

_____

14. Often a baby or an injured adult need to be moved to the Center for more help. _____

_____

15. Marine biologists and other specialists nurses the animal back to health. _____

_____

16. Yasha and Glen wants to volunteer at the Center. _____

_____

Part 3

Write a few sentences about two of your heroes. Make sure the verbs agree with any compound subjects.

_____

_____

_____

_____

_____

_____

_____

Name _____

Unforgettable Folks

Read and Discover

Robyn Davidson traveled alone across Australia's Western Plateau, the **largest** of Australia's three major regions. Preparation took **longer** than the trip itself.

Circle the boldfaced adverb that compares something with one other thing. Underline the boldfaced adjective that compares something with more than one other thing.

The **comparative form** of an **adjective** or an **adverb** compares two people, places, things, or actions. Add *-er* to short adjectives or adverbs to create the comparative form. Use the word *more* before long adjectives and adverbs to create the comparative form (*more careful*). The **superlative form** compares three or more people, places, things, or actions. Add *-est* to create the superlative form. Use the word *most* before long adjectives and adverbs to create the superlative form (*most carefully*). Use the words *better* and *less* to compare two things. Use *best* and *least* to compare three or more things. **Remember to use this information when you speak, too.**

See Handbook Sections 15, 18, and 25

Part 1

Underline the correct form of the adjective or adverb in parentheses.

1. Of the people I've studied, Robyn Davidson is the (more courageous/most courageous).

2. She traveled alone across the Australian outback, a large desert with one of the (harsher/harshest) climates on Earth.

3. During the day, the temperature often soars (higher/highest) than one hundred degrees; at night it drops below zero.

4. These conditions made her journey the (more difficult/most difficult) challenge she faced.

5. However, she also saw amazing things, such as Uluru, the (larger/largest) rock in the world.

6. Davidson trained four camels to carry her supplies; they proved to be even (better/best) friends than her dog, Diggity.

7. Camels are (better/best) than horses for traveling in the desert.

8. As her food diminished, she collected wild onions (more often/most often) than before.

9. As she learned to survive, she felt (wiser/wisest) than when she began her journey.

Unforgettable Folks

Part 2

On the blank, write the correct form of the adjective or adverb in parentheses. (You may need to add *more* or *most*.)

10. After the camels' first escape, Davidson kept them _____ secured. (carefully)

11. Baby Goliath was the _____ of Davidson's four camels. (young)

12. His mother, Zellie, could carry _____ packs than he could. (heavy)

13. Davidson faced many challenges, but the _____ was loneliness. (great)

Part 3

Circle the six hidden adjectives and adverbs. Write the comparative and superlative forms of each word you find.

Q	A	S	L	O	W	L	Y
G	K	H	R	R	M	K	J
T	H	I	R	S	T	Y	S
A	F	W	B	B	H	D	A
F	A	S	T	X	O	Q	N
V	B	G	Q	C	T	K	D
B	R	A	V	E	L	Y	Y

Comparative   Superlative

14. _____ _____

15. _____ _____

16. _____ _____

17. _____ _____

18. _____ _____

19. _____ _____

Name _____

Unforgettable Folks

Read and Discover

John Wesley Powell knew that an expedition down the Colorado River **would be** difficult and dangerous.

He knew he **must find** people with endurance to accompany him. Circle the main verb in boldface in each sentence. Underline the auxiliary verb in boldface that works with each main verb.

An **auxiliary verb,** or **helping verb,** works with a main verb. Auxiliary verbs have different purposes. Some auxiliary verbs such as *could, should, might,* and *may* show how likely it is that something will happen. Some auxiliary verbs such as *did, is, will,* and *would* indicate the tense of the main verb.

See Handbook Section 17

Part 1

Underline the correct form of each verb.

1. John Wesley Powell (is/may) have been America's first environmentalist.

2. When Powell was growing up in the 1830s, his parents and teachers did not know he (would/should) become a well-known naturalist and explorer.

3. They did not know that he (would/should) lead a thousand-mile expedition down the Green and Colorado rivers in 1869.

4. Since no European Americans had charted the Colorado River, Powell and his nine crew members did not know what the journey (would/can) reveal.

5. One thing for certain, they knew they (must/will) complete their journey before their food rations ran out.

6. Powell's team (would/had) travel between the sheer walls of the mile-deep Grand Canyon.

7. Powell felt they (shall/should) move carefully through the strong rapids of the rivers.

8. It (did/may) have been the most exciting expedition in American history.

9. As settlers began to mine and farm the West, Powell said that the U.S. government (does/should) limit development.

10. He warned that careless use of Earth's resources (would/are) lead to disaster.

Unforgettable Folks

Part 2 ✏️

Complete each sentence with the correct auxiliary verb. Some sentences have more than one correct answer.

11. By the time he prepared to explore the West,

    he _____ lost his

    right arm fighting for the Union in the Civil War.

12. This handicap _____ increase

    the difficulty of surviving in the wilderness.

John Wesley Powell knew the value of natural resources.

13. But Powell _____ determined to explore the Colorado River.

14. His love of nature _____ continue to inspire people for

    many generations.

Part 3 ✏️

Decide which auxiliary verb belongs in each clue. Write the verbs in the puzzle.

Across
  2. My mom __ planning our summer vacation now.
  4. In July my family __ travel down the Colorado River in a raft.
  5. Each raft __ have a whitewater expert on board.

Down
  1. We __ invite my cousins to come with us.
  3. Our raft __ flip over in rough waters.
  6. Mom __ tell us we'd have to wear life jackets.

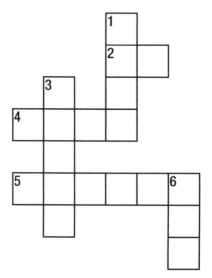

Name _____

Unforgettable Folks

Proofreading Others' Writing

Read this report about the heroes of the 1991 Oakland fire and find the mistakes. Use the proofreading marks below to show how each mistake should be fixed.

Proofreading Marks

Mark	Means	Example
⊙	add a period	Sometimes ordinary people perform heroic acts ⊙
≡	make into a capital letter	<u>s</u>ometimes ordinary people perform heroic acts.
/	make into a lowercase letter	Sometimes ordinary people Perform heroic acts.
ℛ	take away	Sometimes ordinary peoples perform heroic acts.
sp	fix spelling	Sometimes ordanary people perform heroic acts.
∧	add	Sometimes ordinary ∧people perform heroic acts.

Ordinary Heroes

Sometimes in the midst of a tragedy, ordinary people perform heroic actions. In 1991 a huge firestorm rages through California's oakland Hills. Firefighters work around the clock trying to rescue people and prevent homes from burning.

Firefighters from san francisco and other nearby cities helped the Oakland Fire Department A wall of fire threaten to destroy the historic Claremont Hotell. Firefighters saved the hotel, one of the most large wooden buildings in the United States.

During the fire, about one hundred Volunteers assisted the firefighters. Several helped people or animals reach safety; others helped direct traffic, move hoses, or clear brush. When two firefighters fell from a rickety porch, volunteer Nick Bamont rescued they from the fire below. Him and other volunteers whom helped make a big difference. After the fire, neighbors and friends donated food, clothing, and money for the victims and their familys. Their courage and generosity was essential during the days and weeks after the fire.

Proofreading Your Own Writing

You can use the list below to help you find and fix mistakes in your own writing. Write the titles of your own stories or reports in the blanks on top of the chart. Then use the questions to check your work. Make a check mark (✓) in each box after you have checked that item.

Titles

Proofreading Checklist for Unit 4

Have I used subject and object pronouns correctly?				
Have I used pronouns in pairs correctly?				
Have I used *who* and *whom* correctly?				
Do the subject and verb in every sentence agree?				
Have I used comparative forms of adverbs and adjectives correctly?				
Have I used auxiliary verbs correctly?				

Also Remember . . .

Does each sentence begin with a capital letter?				
Does each sentence end with the right mark?				
Have I spelled each word correctly?				
Have I used commas correctly?				

Your Own List
Use this space to write your own list of things to check in your writing.

Name _____

Unforgettable Your Folks

Pronouns

Circle each boldfaced word that is a subject pronoun. Underline each boldfaced word that is an object pronoun. (1–5)

Jonas Salk developed the first polio vaccine. **He** saved thousands of lives. Salk's wife and sons helped **him**. **They** were the first people to receive the vaccine. Polio had claimed many lives. **It** was a deadly disease. Salk received many awards for his work, but **he** never accepted prize money.

Circle the correct pronoun or pronouns in parentheses.

6. Chantal and (me/I) are making a "heroes hall of fame."

7. My father drove (us/we) to the library to learn about more heroes to add to our collection.

8. (She and I/Her and I) went to talk with the librarian, Mr. Wohl.

9. We asked (he/him) to help us begin our research.

Circle the antecedent of each boldfaced pronoun.

10. He showed us a book about Nobel Prize winners. **It** was a great place to start.

11. As Chantal and I read, **we** learned that some of the world's greatest heroes have received these prizes.

12. Nobel Prizes are awarded each year. **They** are given to recognize outstanding accomplishments in science, economics, literature, and world peace.

Who and *Whom*

Write *who* or *whom* to complete each sentence correctly.

13. Chantal and I enjoyed reading about these and other people with _____ we had been unfamiliar.

14. _____ will win Nobel Prizes next year?

15. The judges _____ choose the winners meet in Norway and Sweden.

16. Each winner receives about $800,000 and a medal with a picture of Alfred Nobel, for _____ the prize is named.

Verbs

Circle the correct form of each verb in parentheses.

17. Swedish chemist Alfred Nobel (begins/began) the awards around 1900.

18. The first prizes (was/were) awarded in 1901.

19. In the coming years, prizes (would/had) go to outstanding scientists, writers, and peacemakers.

20. Alfred Nobel said that in order to win a prize, the nominee's work (should/do) contribute to the "good of humanity."

21. A writer or a scientist (give/gives) much to the world.

22. The efforts of Nobel Prize winners Octavio Paz and Nelson Mandela (has/have) contributed to humanity in many ways.

23. Paz's poems and essays (enrich/enriches) readers' lives.

24. Mandela's work in South Africa (helps/helped) end the brutal system of apartheid.

25. For decades, apartheid (deprive/had deprived) nonwhite people of many human rights.

Adjectives and Adverbs

Complete each sentence by circling the correct form of the adjective or adverb in parentheses.

26. Some of the (more significant/most significant) achievements of recent times have been rewarded Nobel Prizes.

27. But many prize winners feel that the (greater/greatest) reward of all is watching their work benefit others.

28. Some winners are (less/least) well-known than others.

29. But all of them have made the world a (best/better) place.

30. Chantal and I may have to make our "heroes hall of fame" (larger/largest) than we had planned.

Name _____

Unforgettable Folks

FAMILY LEARNING OPPORTUNITIES

In Unit 4 of *G.U.M.* we are learning how different kinds of words are used in sentences. The activities on these pages give extra practice with some of these concepts. You can help reinforce the information your son or daughter is learning in school by choosing one or more activities to complete at home.

Compare/Contrast (Comparing with Adjectives and Adverbs)

Have your son or daughter think of a type of object that both of you own, such as a sweater, a T-shirt, a toothbrush, or a bicycle. Then have him or her write three sentences comparing the two things. Ask your son or daughter to underline the word or words that compare.

Examples	Your bicycle is <u>shinier</u> than mine.
	My bike's horn can honk <u>more</u> <u>loudly</u> than yours.
	Your T-shirt is <u>cleaner</u> than mine.
	My T-shirt is <u>more</u> <u>raggedy</u> than yours.

Who Said What to Whom? (Subject and Object Pronouns)

Ask your child to think of a person or an object that is familiar to both of you. Then have your child write two sentences about that object using pronouns; ask him or her not to name the object.

Example	Uncle Ira roasts (it) for (us) in November. (You) eat (it) with stuffing, yams, and mashed potatoes.

Read the sentences and try to guess who the secret person is or what the secret object is. After you have guessed, work with your child to circle each pronoun he or she used.

The Ways We Were (Forms of *Be*)

With your child, flip through old yearbooks or a family photo album. Have your child select three or four pictures and write captions for them, using forms of the verb *be*, such as *am, is, are, was,* or *were.*

Example	Mom **is** next to Aunt Rosie. Their brother Mike **is** on Mom's other side. This picture was taken in the summertime, when they **were** all at the lake.

After your child has completed writing the captions, check the sentences together to make sure the forms of *be* have been used correctly.

Imagine This **(Making the Subject and Verb Agree)**

Work with your child to think of three subjects, three verbs, and three locations. (Or, use the list below.) Write them in three columns, like this:

A huge green kangaroo	slither	a mud puddle.
Eight orange soda cans	stride	the library.
The pink poodles	scuttle	the aisle.

Then ask your child to choose one word or phrase from each column and write a silly sentence. He or she should change word forms as necessary to make the sentence correct. Make sure the verb agrees with the subject.

> **Example**   Eight orange soda cans scuttle into the library.

Sixth Graders of Yesteryear **(Pronouns in Pairs)**

Ask your child to interview you (or another adult) about an adventure you had with a friend when you were in the sixth grade. Encourage your child to take notes during the interview. Then have your child write four sentences describing what you and your friend did, using pronouns in some of the sentences.

> **Example**   Dad and Ed Graham were best friends. **He** and **Dad** used to play in a band together. Once their school asked **Dad** and **him** to play for a school assembly.

Read the completed sentences aloud together. Make sure the pronouns have been used correctly.

Name _____

Unforgettable Folks

Read  and Discover

   a. Wow, these stones are huge!
   b. What were they used for?
   c. No one knows their original purpose.
   d. Listen to these facts about Stonehenge.

Which sentence gives a command? _____ Circle its end mark.
Which sentence shows excitement? _____ Circle its end mark.
Which sentence asks a question? _____ Circle its end mark.
Which sentence makes a statement? _____ Circle its end mark.

Begin every **sentence** with a capital letter. A **declarative** sentence makes a statement and ends with a **period**. An **interrogative** sentence asks a question and ends with a **question mark**. An **imperative** sentence gives a command and ends with a **period** or an **exclamation point**. An **exclamatory** sentence shows excitement and ends with an **exclamation point**.

See Handbook Section 9

Part 1

Each sentence is either declarative (DE), interrogative (INT), imperative (IMP), or exclamatory (EX). Label each sentence with *DE, INT, IMP,* or *EX.*

1. Stonehenge is an ancient circle of huge stones on England's Salisbury Plain. _____

2. Where does the name *Stonehenge* come from? _____

3. It is from a French phrase meaning "hanging stones," because the stones seem to hang in the air. _____

4. Hey, this guidebook says that Stonehenge is one of the world's oldest monuments! _____

   Most historians believe Stonehenge is a product of the Bronze Age.

5. Archaeologists believe it was completed about 1500 B.C. _____

6. Tell me why Stonehenge was built. _____

7. Did you know that Stonehenge's main axis is aligned with the midsummer sunrise? _____

8. Some astronomers think the stones were used to predict eclipses. _____

9. Other people think Stonehenge was used for religious ceremonies. _____

10. Wow, some historians think it took 300 years to build Stonehenge! _____

Part 2

Draw three lines (≡) under each lowercase letter that should be capitalized. Then add correct end marks.

11. Look at the lintel stones, the flat stones lying across the vertical stones

12. how did the builders put the lintel stones in place

13. they may have built ramps and pulled the stone slabs up the slope

14. What incredibly hard work it must have been

15. wow, some of the stones weigh thirty tons

16. Has anyone ever estimated how long it took to build Stonehenge

17. one historian added up all the tasks, including digging ditches, cutting and carrying

stone, and putting stones in place

18. He estimated that it took 1.5 million workdays to build Stonehenge

Part 3

In the space below, design a travel poster to entice tourists to visit Stonehenge. Use the four kinds of sentences in your poster.

Name

Looking Back

Read  and Discover

Leif Erikson was the first European sailor to reach North America. He built a community in what is now Canada nearly 500 years before Columbus landed in the Americas.

Circle words that name specific people, places, or things.

> A common noun names a person, place, thing, or idea. A **proper noun** names a specific person, place, thing, or idea. The important words in proper nouns are **capitalized**. **Proper adjectives** are descriptive words formed from proper nouns. They must be capitalized. A **title of respect**, such as *Mr.* or *Judge*, is used before a person's name. It is also capitalized.

See Handbook Sections 1, 14, and 15

Part 1

Circle lowercase letters that should be capital letters. Draw a line through capital letters that should be lowercase. (1–16)

Leif Erikson was born in iceland about A.D. 960. His father was named erik the Red. Erik had moved to Iceland from norway. After a Series of fights, Erik the red was banished from Iceland for three years. Banishment was a common punishment in ancient icelandic society.

A skilled Norse sailor, Erik the Red decided to spend his banishment investigating reports of Islands off Iceland's west coast. Erik sailed across the atlantic in an open boat called a *knörr*. In July of that year, Erik reached a huge, uninhabited Island mostly covered by ice. However, the island's southwestern coast was ice-free and fertile. Erik named this land greenland.

When Erik returned to Iceland, he told tales of a rich land to the west. The next summer he returned to Greenland with a group of icelandic settlers. These people became Greenland's first European community. Leif erikson was among them. Erik named the community brattahild. For 14 years the Greenland colony grew, but problems persisted. Supplies had to be shipped from norway, and Greenland's limited supply of timber was rapidly being depleted. Leif Erikson set out to search for a "heavily wooded land" to the west, which a sailor named bjarni had described. That land was North america.

Part 2

Rewrite these sentences to correct the errors.

17. leif's crew sailed northwest, passing what is known today as baffin island, canada.

_____

_____

18. They eventually landed near where a River met the atlantic ocean. _____

_____

19. The greenlanders were impressed with the thick forests, the mild Weather, and the giant

salmon in the streams. _____

_____

20. They stayed through the winter, and when they left for greenland in the spring Leif

named this land vinland. _____

_____

21. The small community they founded is believed to have been the first european settlement

in north america. _____

_____

Part 3

Imagine you were on Leif's crew. Write a note to your parents. Describe the voyage and the settlement you founded. Use at least three proper nouns and two proper adjectives.

_____

_____

_____

_____

Name _____

Looking Back

Read  and Discover

Our class invited Dr. Nick L. Tucker, an archaeologist, to visit us. Our teacher, Mrs. Willis, made the arrangements. She posted a sign that said: "Mon., Feb. 23—2:30 p.m.—Dr. Tucker."

Underline a short way to write Doctor. *Draw a square around a short way to write* Mistress. *Circle short ways to write* Monday *and* February. *Underline a letter that stands for a name.*

An **abbreviation** is a shortened form of a word. **Titles of respect** are usually abbreviated. So are words in **addresses** like *Street* (*St.*), *Avenue* (*Ave.*), and *Boulevard* (*Blvd.*). **Days,** some **months,** and parts of **business names** (*Co. for Company*) are often abbreviated in informal notes. Abbreviations usually begin with a capital letter and end with a period. An **initial** can replace a person's or a place's name. It is written as a capital letter followed by a period.

See Handbook Section 2

Part 1

Circle each lowercase letter that should be a capital letter. Draw a line through each capital letter that should be a lowercase letter. Add periods where they are needed. (1–14)

Dr Nick L Tucker spoke about ancient Egypt and about the discovery of King Tutankhamun's tomb. King Tut was an Egyptian pharaoh who died at the age of 18 or 19. His Tomb lay hidden for more than 3,000 years in Egypt's Valley of the Kings.

King Tut ruled Egypt 3,000 years ago.

The tomb was first discovered by dr. Howard Carter, an Egyptologist, and a British nobleman named Lord Carnarvon. These two explorers discovered the tomb on november 26, 1922.

The discovery of King Tut's tomb astonished the world. Our History teacher, mr. Kale, told us that thousands of artifacts were found. Mr Kale said that it took archaeologists ten years to remove them. Many items were crafted of solid gold, alabaster, or a deep blue stone called lapis lazuli.

Dr Tucker brought photographs from his office on Baker blvd. Some showed golden shrines, King Tut's throne, and two life-sized statues of the Boy king.

Dr. Tucker is helping us prepare our own display about King Tut. Our project will be shown in April at the library on Drake st. The Cecil B Grant corp. is helping to fund our project.

Looking Back

Part 2

Rewrite this announcement on the lines. Use abbreviations and initials where you can.

> The Sixth Grade Class of
> Doctor Martin Luther King, Junior, School
> PRESENTS
> **"The Mysteries of King Tut"**
> Monday, February 7–Wednesday, February 28
> Hubert Paul Grant Library
> 4243 Drake Street
> **Consultant:** Doctor Nick Lloyd Tucker

_____

_____

_____

_____

_____

_____

_____

_____

Part 3

Pretend you are an Egyptologist. Design a business card for yourself below. Include your name, home address, and phone number. Use initials and abbreviations when you can.

Name _____

Looking Back

Read and Discover

My class watched a movie titled <u>The Valley of the Kings</u>. We also read a story called "Mummy Mysteries."

Circle the movie title. Draw a box around the story title. How are they written differently? _____

_____

> Underline **book titles** and **movie titles**. Use quotation marks around the titles of **songs, stories,** and **poems. Capitalize** the first word and last word in titles. Capitalize all other words except articles, prepositions, and conjunctions. Remember to capitalize short verbs, such as *is* and *are*.
>
> **See Handbook Section 3**

Part 1

Circle each lowercase letter that should be a capital letter. Underline and add quotation marks where you need to.

1. My favorite book about ancient Egypt is titled egyptian kingdoms of long ago.

2. Deke wrote a story titled on the mummy trail.

3. Deke and I made up a song called the king tut shuffle.

4. I wrote a poem called the pharaoh's dream, and I entered it in a poetry contest.

5. My poem may be selected to appear in a book titled young voices.

6. Deke and I rented the movie pyramids of the sun.

7. We loved the theme song, nile journey.

8. The movie was based on a book titled in search of the lost kings.

9. Deke lent me a book of mysteries called the hissing of the snake.

10. My favorite story in the book is called the mummy's revenge.

11. My poem felines in the palace is about the importance of cats in ancient Egyptian society.

12. I want to rent the movie pharaohs of fire.

13. I was a boy king is the title of a story told from King Tut's point of view.

14. Deke and I plan to write our own book about the pharaohs, titled the pyramid kings.

Part 2

Read the titles of the works on the library shelf and then answer each question. Use correct capitalization and punctuation.

15. Which book probably contains information about Egypt's natural environment?

_____

16. Which book is most likely a suspenseful adventure story? _____

_____

17. Which movie probably gives information about tools used to study ancient civilizations?

_____

18. Which book is most likely to be humorous? _____

_____

19. Which movie is probably science fiction? _____

_____

Part 3

Think of a story, book, or movie you would like to create about ancient Egypt. Write the title and a brief description of it. Check your title for correct punctuation and capitalization.

Title: _____

_____

_____

Name _____

Looking Back

Read and Discover

Earth's geography has changed greatly over time. Geologists believe that a land bridge once connected Asia and North America. Historians **don't** agree on the date this bridge was formed.

Which boldfaced word shows possession or ownership? _____

Which boldfaced word is a combination of two words? _____

> To form the **possessive** of a singular noun, add an **apostrophe** and *s* (*girl's shoe*). For plural nouns that end in *s*, add an apostrophe (*birds' nests*). For plural nouns that do not end in *s*, add an apostrophe and *s* (*children's boots*). **Apostrophes** are also used in **contractions,** two words that have been shortened and combined.
>
> See Handbook Sections 7, 24, 26, and 28

Part 1

Circle the correct word in parentheses. If the answer is a possessive, write *possessive*. If the answer is a contraction, write the two words the contraction was made from.

1. (Archaeologists'/Archaeologist's) studies show that human beings first lived in North America in about 9500 B.C. _____

2. These hunters and gatherers (didn't/did'nt) have fancy tools or weapons. _____

3. Prehistoric (hunter's/hunters') prey included mammoths, ground sloths, and other giants of the Ice Age. _____

4. A (hunter's/hunters') tools included stone points, spears, and knives. _____

5. Historians think that the crude stone weapons found at hunting sites (weren't/were'nt) strong enough to pierce the thick hides of the mammoth. _____

6. They believe that early (peoples/peoples') hunting methods more commonly included forcing herds of animals off cliffs. _____

7. Early North Americans (did'nt/didn't) rely on big game for their survival. _____

8. Seeds, plants, snails, and rabbits were also part of a prehistoric (families/family's) diet. _____

9. The West (Coast's/Coasts') first inhabitants probably relied on gathering fruits and seeds instead of hunting. _____

Part 2

Rewrite these sentences. Replace boldfaced words with possessives or contractions.

10. The **oldest shoe in the world** was discovered in a cave in Oregon. _____

_____

11. **It is** woven of shredded rope made of sagebrush. _____

_____

12. The **dry climate of the cave** preserved this sandal for more than 9,000 years! _____

_____

13. The first Americans **did not** have knowledge of pottery making, metalworking, or

agriculture. _____

_____

14. **The early inhabitants of North America** would not develop these skills for thousands of

years. _____

_____

Part 3

Circle the six hidden words in the puzzle. Write the possessive form of each noun and the contraction of each verb.

Q	P	Q	F	I	D	W	Q	S	K	R
Z	E	F	K	S	H	E	L	T	E	R
W	O	M	E	N	Q	R	K	D	L	P
T	P	G	L	O	M	E	R	X	Z	M
Q	L	H	Z	T	B	N	T	G	X	N
R	E	J	X	C	V	O	Y	H	C	B
S	C	A	N	N	O	T	K	J	V	V

15. _____

16. _____

17. _____

18. _____

19. _____

20. _____

Read and Discover

a. The Great Wall of China, the longest wall in the world, is the only human creation that can be seen from space.
b. The Great Wall of China is built of stone, earth, and brick.

Circle the commas in sentence a. Circle the commas in sentence b. In which sentence do the commas separate three items in a series? _____

A **series** is a list of three or more words or phrases. **Commas** are used to separate items in a series. Each item in a series might consist of one word or a longer phrase. The last comma in a series goes before the conjunction (*and, or*). A comma is not needed to separate two items.

See Handbook Section 8

Part 1

Add commas where they are needed in the sentences. Cross out commas that should not be there.

1. Long ago, warring Chinese states built walls to protect their crops cattle and, communities from each other.

2. These early walls were crude uneven and often hastily constructed.

3. In about 221 B.C., the king of Qin took control of the warring states united them and named himself the first emperor of China.

4. This ruler called for the existing walls to be expanded strengthened and, consolidated into a single wall.

5. The wall was built mostly by soldiers prisoners and, peasants; its construction took hundreds of years.

6. The wall itself could not fight enemies, and protect citizens.

7. Watchtowers fortresses and living quarters were built at strategic points along the wall.

8. The fortresses housed troops supplies and weapons.

9. Soldiers had to guard the wall fight off enemies maintain the towers, and grow food.

10. Soldiers used fire smoke and, flag signals to communicate with each other.

11. Soldiers' letters complained about the low pay poor living conditions and isolation of life.

The Great Wall of China is visible from the moon.

Looking Back

Part 2 ✏️

Rewrite each group of sentences as a single sentence. Use *and* or *or* to join the last two items in a series.

12. Some visitors have taken bits of the Great Wall.
    Some visitors have written their names on the Great Wall.
    Visitors have worn down sections of the Great Wall.

    _____

    _____

    _____

13. Some parts of the Great Wall have single walls.
    Some parts of the Great Wall have double walls.
    Some parts of the Great Wall have triple walls.

    _____

    _____

    _____

14. The Great Wall is constructed of unfired brick.   The Great Wall is constructed of rock.
    The Great Wall is constructed of stone.   The Great Wall is constructed of earth.

    _____

    _____

    _____

Part 3 ✏️

Imagine that you are a soldier living on China's Great Wall in ancient times. Write a journal entry about an experience. Use items in a series in one sentence, and use commas correctly.

_____

_____

_____

_____

Name _____

Looking 🌐 Back

Read  and Discover

"Mrs. Perez, is it true that huge cities existed in Mexico thousands of years ago?" David asked.

"Yes, Tenochtitlán was Mexico's largest ancient city, and as many as 200,000 people may have lived there."

Find the name of the person being spoken to in the first sentence. What punctuation mark comes after it? _____

Find the word that introduces the second sentence. What punctuation mark follows it? _____

Find the conjunction that joins the two parts of the second sentence. What punctuation mark comes before it? _____

Commas tell a reader where to pause. A comma is used to separate an **introductory word** from the rest of a sentence. It is used to separate **independent clauses** in a **compound sentence** and to separate a **noun of direct address** from the rest of a sentence. A noun of direct address names a person who is being spoken to.

See Handbook Sections 8 and 21

Part 1

Add the missing comma to each sentence. Then decide why the comma is needed. Write *I* for introductory word, *C* for compound sentence, or *D* for direct address.

1. "Hey listen to this!" Emil said. ___

2. "About 40,000 people lived in the city of Teotihuacán in 100 B.C. and by A.D. 500 its population had tripled!" ___

3. "Was this city similar to modern cities Mrs. Perez?" asked Amy. ___

4. "Well Teotihuacán had about 2,000 apartment houses," Mrs. Perez answered. ___

5. "It also had a huge open market and archaeologists have identified 500 workshops." ___

6. "Yes I see some similarities," Hank noted. ___

7. "I can picture the appearance of an ancient city but I can't imagine a big city without electricity," Duane said. ___

8. "Duane did you know that Teotihuacán had more than 600 pyramids?" asked Emil. ___

9. "They were all impressive but the Pyramid of the Sun is the most famous one," Mrs. Perez said. ___

Part 2 ✏

Rewrite the sentences, adding the words in parentheses. Be sure to use commas correctly.

10. The Aztecs also built an enormous city in Mexico. (and) They named it Tenochtitlán.

_____

_____

11. The Aztecs were keen observers of astronomy. (and) They developed a 365-day solar

calendar. _____

_____

12. The Aztecs ruled an entire empire. (but) The conquest by European explorer Hernando

Cortés in 1521 brought their empire to an end. _____

_____

_____

Part 3 ✏

Use the information in this lesson to figure out the answer to each riddle. Then use the numbered letters to find the name of a famous Aztec ruler.

13. About 2,000 of these were discovered in Teotihuacán.

___ ___ ___ ___ ___ ___ ___   ___ ___ ___ ___ ___
     4 1   3   7

14. His army defeated the Aztecs in 1521. ___ ___ ___ ___ ___ ___
       2   5

15. Mexicans and Egyptians both constructed these. ___ ___ ___ ___ ___ ___ ___ ___
           8

16. These people once ruled an empire. ___ ___ ___ ___ ___ ___
   9 6

Who was one of the Aztec empire's most famous rulers? ___ ___ ___ ___ ___ ___ ___ ___ ___
        1 2 3 4 5 6 7 8 9

Name _____

Looking Back

Read  and Discover

   a. In 1982 a young Turkish diver saw strange objects on the ocean floor, he'd never seen anything like them.

   b. The diver knew what to do: he told his captain.

   c. The diver described the objects as "metal biscuits with ears"; his captain guessed they were Bronze Age copper ingots.

In which sentence are two independent clauses separated incorrectly with only a comma? _____ What marks are used to separate the independent clauses in the other two sentences? _____ and _____

> A **semicolon** can be used instead of a comma and conjunction to separate the independent clauses in a **compound sentence**. A **colon** can be used to separate two sentences when the second sentence states a direct result of the first.

See Handbook Section 8

Part 1

Write a colon or a semicolon to separate the clauses in each sentence. Sentences 4, 6, and 9 require a colon.

1. In 1982 a shipwreck was discovered off the coast of Turkey it was the oldest shipwreck found.

2. Divers named the ship *Ulu Burun* it held artifacts from seven ancient cultures.

3. The *Ulu Burun* sank in the fourteenth century B.C. it sat on the ocean floor for 34 centuries.

4. The wreck gave archaeologists an amazing opportunity it provided a glimpse into the trade routes and cargoes of the ancient Mediterranean.

5. Archaeologists found huge jars called *pithos* drawings of these jars appear on the walls of Egyptian tombs.

6. The cargo included many kinds of raw materials copper, tin, and ivory were among them.

7. The ship carried six tons of copper the copper would be mixed with tin to make bronze.

8. The copper was in the form of ingots each weighed about 60 pounds.

9. Finished goods were also found pottery, gold jewelry, and bronze swords were among them.

10. The treasures included ebony from Africa amber from northern Europe was also found.

11. During the fourteenth century B.C., pharaohs ruled Egypt many artifacts from the *Ulu Burun* are Egyptian.

Looking Back

Part 2 ✏️

Each sentence on the left can be matched with a sentence on the right to make a compound sentence. Draw a line to match sentences. Then rewrite each pair of sentences as one sentence. Use a semicolon or a colon to separate independent clauses.

About 5,000 years ago metalworkers discovered that copper and tin could be melted together.

The Bronze Age changed the world dramatically.

Shipbuilders built faster, stronger ships.

Trade routes expanded.

Superior bronze tools made farming, ship-building, and many other jobs much easier.

The ships carried bigger cargoes farther distances.

Cultures met and exchanged ideas.

This combination of metals produces bronze.

12. _____

_____

13. _____

_____

14. _____

_____

15. _____

_____

Part 3 ✏️

Imagine that the treasures of the *Ulu Burun* will be displayed in your community. Write an announcement describing the exhibit for your newspaper. Include two compound sentences.

_____

_____

_____

Name _____

Looking Back

Read and Discover

Marcus asked, "Can you tell me about the African empire of Ghana?" Martin explained that Ghana was the first great African empire. Which sentence shows a speaker's exact words? Underline it. Circle the marks that begin and end this quotation. Circle the first letter of the quotation.

A **direct quotation** is a speaker's exact words. Use **quotation marks** at the beginning and end of a direct quotation. Use a comma to separate the speaker's exact words from the rest of the sentence. Begin a direct quotation with a capital letter. Add end punctuation before the last quotation mark. An **indirect quotation** is a retelling of a speaker's words. Do not use quotation marks when the word *that* or *whether* comes before a speaker's words.

See Handbook Section 4

Part 1

Write *I* after each indirect quotation and *D* after each direct quotation. Then add quotation marks, commas, and end marks to direct quotations. Draw three lines (≡) under lowercase letters that should be capitalized.

1. Marcus asked when did the empire of Ghana flourish? ____

2. Martin said that it began in about A.D. 700 and reached its height in about A.D. 1000. ____

3. Anton asked what caused the empire to grow? ____

4. Martin explained that the people had a vast supply of gold and many iron weapons that enabled them to defend their territory. ____

5. The capital city of Kumbi became the center of trade in West Africa, he continued. ____

6. He said that the markets of Kumbi were bustling with traders. ____

7. I've heard that Ghana is famous for gold Kevin said. ____

8. One traveler visited the king of Ghana and recorded the wonders he saw Kevin said. ____

9. Martin explained that Ghana lacked its own supply of salt and that salt was essential for survival in the desert. ____

10. By some reports, gold and salt were traded in equal weight, he explained. ____

Ghana was the world's main source of gold.

Looking Back

Part 2 ✏️

Rewrite each indirect quotation as a direct quotation. Rewrite each direct quotation as an indirect quotation. (There is more than one right way to do this.) Be sure to use punctuation marks correctly.

11. "What we know about Ghana is based largely on the writings of the traders who visited it," Martin said. _____

_____

12. "In A.D. 1203, Ghana was defeated by an army from North Africa," Martin explained.

_____

_____

13. He said that Ghana became part of the kingdom of Mali, Africa's second great empire.

_____

_____

Part 3 ✏️

Imagine you are a trader in ancient Kumbi. In the first box, draw yourself and the trade item you have brought. In the second, draw the item you want in exchange and the person trading it. Under each box write direct quotations of what you might say to each other.

_____   _____

_____   _____

Name _____

Looking Back

Read  and Discover

Point Reyes National Seashore
Point Reyes, California 94956
July 30, 1997

Dear Paula,
    Point Reyes is beautiful. My family's campsite is by a stream. Yesterday we visited Miwok Village, a model of a Coast Miwok community.
                    Your friend,
                    (Lia)

There are five different parts of this letter. Two have already been circled. Circle the other three.

> A **friendly letter** has five parts. The **heading** gives your address and the date. The **greeting** includes the name of the person to whom you are writing. It begins with a capital letter and ends with a comma. The **body** gives your message. The **closing** is a friendly way to say good-bye. It ends with a comma. The **signature** is your name. A friendly letter is written to someone you know and may include informal language.
> A **business letter** is a formal letter written to an employer or a business. It has the same parts as a friendly letter, but it also includes the complete address of the person you are writing to. In a business letter, write a colon after the greeting.

See Handbook Sections 31 and 32

Part 1

Label the five parts of the friendly letter below. Write the name of each part on the line next to it. (1–5)

                            2422 Cherrywood Lane

_____ Plymouth, Michigan 48170

                            August 15, 1997

Dear Lia, _____

    Camp was great. I learned to ride a horse and cook stew over a fire. I liked everything about

camp except the mosquitoes! _____

                          Your friend, _____

                          Paula _____

Part 2

Rewrite this business letter correctly on the lines below. (Hint: The sender's address and the date go on the right. The business's address goes on the left.)

Sundance Publishing 4355 Fifth Avenue New York, NY 10001 Dear Sir or Madam: August 3, 1997 I am interested in books about Native American cultures in the United States. Please send me a catalog of your publications. Sincerely, Anna Ross 443 Oak Street San Antonio, TX 78265

_____

_____

_____

_____

_____

_____

_____

_____

_____

_____

_____

_____

_____

Part 3

Circle the five parts of a friendly letter in this word search.

G	R	E	E	T	I	N	G	T	B	Q	X	N	E
B	V	Z	Q	A	V	J	C	L	O	S	I	N	G
H	E	A	D	I	N	G	I	A	D	E	M	R	T
D	T	B	E	K	P	U	L	X	Y	Q	W	P	H
S	I	G	N	A	T	U	R	E	V	T	S	K	L

Name _____

Looking Back

Proofreading Others' Writing

Read this letter about archaeology and find the mistakes. Use the proofreading marks below to show how each mistake should be fixed.

Proofreading Marks

Mark	Means	Example
≡	make into a capital letter	"Be careful with that vase!" i said.
/	make into a lowercase letter	"Be careful with that vase!" I Said.
⊙	add a period	"Be careful with that vase!" I said⊙
⋏	add a comma	I said⋏ "Be careful!"
ⱽ	add quotation marks	ⱽBe careful with that vase!" I said.
sp	fix spelling	"Be careful with that vace!" I said.
ⱽ	add apostrophe	"Dont drop it!"

Archaeology Institute

43 Ridge Rd

Santa Fe, New Mexico 87501

August 15 1997

Dear Jay

Your mom asked me to tell you about archaeology. Ive been an archaeologist for ten years.

Archaeologists use physical clues to learn about people who didn't leave no written records. We study three kinds of cluse *artifacts, features,* and *ecofacts.* Artifacts are objects that are made by people and can be removed, such as jewelry copper ingots and Pottery. Features are large structures built by people, such as Chinas Great Wall. Ecofacts are objects like bones found at prehistoric sites.

An archaeologists challenge is locating a site to study. Some, like Stonehenge, are aboveground. Some such as King Tut's tomb, are buried underground. Others such as *Ulu Burun* are underwater. Archaeologists often search for years for certain sites. in 1940 children stumbled upon the entrance to a cave in france. This cave has the finest examples of prehistoric wall paintings ever discovered?

Dr. E f grey said, an archaeologist's best tool is patience." Sometimes discovery takes a long time.

I've enclosed my copy of Dr Grey's latest book, Understanding pictographs. I hope you'll like it

Sincerely

Uncle Roger

Proofreading Your Own Writing

You can use the list below to help you find and fix mistakes in your own writing. Write the titles of your own stories or reports in the blanks on top of the chart. Then use the questions to check your work. Make a check mark (✓) in each box after you have checked that item.

Titles

Proofreading Checklist for Unit 5

Have I capitalized proper nouns, proper adjectives, and all the important words in titles?				
Have I placed quotation marks around direct quotations?				
Have I used commas to separate items in a series and after introductory words?				
Have I joined each compound sentence with a comma and a conjunction, a colon, or a semicolon?				

Also Remember . . .

Does each sentence begin with a capital letter and end with the right end mark?				
Do all abbreviations begin with a capital letter and end with a period?				
Have I used possessives correctly?				
Have I used contractions correctly?				

Your Own List

Use this space to write your own list of things to check in your writing.

Name _____

Looking Back

Punctuation and Capitalization

Cross out incorrect punctuation and add correct punctuation. Draw three lines (≡) under each letter that should be capitalized. Then label each sentence *declarative, interrogative, imperative,* or *exclamatory.*

1. What do archaeologists do after they have discovered a site. _____

2. they must count and photograph each item they find? _____

3. What a painstaking job _____

4. some artifacts fall apart when they come in contact with air? _____

5. consider archaeology as a career _____

Draw three lines under each letter that should be capitalized. Add underlines, quotation marks, and periods where they are needed.

6. the first archaeological digs were conducted by wealthy european explorers.

7. During the 1700s people began to collect artifacts from ancient greece and Rome.

8. The english scholar sir flinders petrie was a pioneer in the field of archaeology.

9. Sir flinders saw the value in everyday objects, not just in treasures made of gold.

10. I read a book about archaeology titled Digging up the past.

11. It was written by Dr r f Callahan.

12. My class watched a movie titled on the trail of troy.

13. I wrote a story titled ghana's golden past.

Apostrophes

Underline the correct word in each pair. Write *C* if the word is a contraction and *P* if the word is a possessive.

14. What can tools tell us about a (people's/peoples') way of life? _____

15. The materials used to make tools reveal a (culture's/cultures') technological skill. _____

16. Bronze tools (were'nt/weren't) widely used until about 5,000 years ago. _____

17. Most ancient cultures (did'nt/didn't) leave written records behind. _____

Commas, Semicolons, and Colons

Add commas, semicolons, or colons where they are needed. (Item 21 requires a colon.)

18. The first archaeological digs took place in Greece France Egypt Iraq and Turkey.

19. "Yes remains were found in many European countries," she replied.

20. Cave paintings were found in France the remains of an ancient site were found in Greece.

21. These findings proved one thing people have lived in Europe for thousands of years.

Quotations

Write *D* after each direct quotation and *I* after each indirect quotation. Add quotation marks and other marks as needed. Draw three lines (≡) under each letter that should be capitalized.

22. What traits do archaeologists need? Kim asked Mrs. Fey. ____

23. Mrs. Fey answered this work requires patience and curiosity. ____

24. Kim said that she is interested in archaeology as a career. ____

Business Letter

Rewrite this business letter correctly on the blanks.

25. Dear Sir or Madam: Digging Supplies Unlimited 434 Brook Street Bakersfield, CA 93302 Please send me your latest catalog. Lisa M. Rojas 224 Elm Avenue Madison, WI 53714 September 18, 1997 Sincerely yours,

_____

_____

_____

_____

_____

_____

_____

_____

_____

Name _____

Looking Back

FAMILY LEARNING OPPORTUNITIES

In Unit 5 of *G.U.M.* we are learning which letters to capitalize and how to use punctuation marks such as periods, commas, and quotation marks. The activities on this page give extra practice with some of the concepts we're learning. You can reinforce this information by choosing one or more activities to complete with your son or daughter at home.

Word Search (Apostrophes)

Work with your son or daughter to find the ten words hidden in the word search. Then ask your son or daughter to write as many contractions as he or she can form by combining these words in different ways. (For example, *don't* is formed by combining *do* and *not*.)

```
W  X  Y  I  S  T  X
I  E  O  Q  E  H  E
L  S  U  V  Q  E  N
L  H  W  A  S  Y  O
W  E  A  R  E  V  T
```

Design a Postcard (Proper Nouns and Proper Adjectives; Initials and Abbreviations)

Help your son or daughter use blank index cards to design his or her own postcard. Follow these steps:

1. Draw a picture on one side of the card.
2. Draw a line down the middle of the back of the card, and write a message on the left side of the line.
3. Write the address of a friend or a family member on the right side.

Remind your son or daughter to capitalize proper nouns and to use abbreviations such as *St.* and *Ave.* in the address. Encourage him or her to stamp and mail the card.

The Critics Speak (Titles)

Ask your son or daughter to write a short review of a favorite book, movie, or song. Then ask him or her to write a review of a least favorite book, movie, or song. Invite your child to be specific about what he or she liked or disliked. Also, remind him or her to capitalize all the important words in a title, to underline book and movie titles, and to use quotation marks around the titles of songs.

In the News (Commas in a Series; Direct and Indirect Quotations)

Use a section of your local paper for a scavenger hunt. See who can be the first to find an example of each item below:

Item	Example
comma in a series	The quarterback faked to the left, stepped back, and threw the ball.
direct quotation	He said, "I just relaxed and concentrated on the game."
indirect quotation	The coach said that the team was well prepared.

Whose Is Whose? (Apostrophes)

Help your child make and decorate self-sticking labels for other family members. Make sure he or she uses apostrophes correctly. Other family members might use the labels on notebooks, crayon boxes, toy or tool boxes, or other items.

Examples	Jenine's Notebook
	The Twins' Crayons
	Dad's Tools

Pen Pal (Friendly Letters and Business Letters)

Encourage your son or daughter to begin a correspondence with a pen pal. Help him or her find a pen pal using an organization such as Pen Pals Unlimited (P.O. Box 6283, Huntington Beach, CA 92615). Remind your son or daughter to use the friendly letter form when writing to the pen pal.

Name _____

Looking Back

Extra Practice

Lesson 1 Circle the complete subject in each sentence. Underline the complete predicate.

1. The Chinese invented kites around 1200 B.C.

2. The military sent messages with them.

3. Some kites looked like birds.

4. Some people used kites as aircraft.

5. Bamboo rods formed the frames.

6. Paper made the kites lightweight.

7. The wind carried people through the air.

8. Hand grips were important.

9. Hang gliders resemble these ancient flying machines.

10. Kite construction also influenced airplane design.

Lesson 2 Circle the simple subject in each sentence. If the understood subject is *you*, write *you* on the line. Underline the simple predicate.

1. My grandmother decorates eggs as a hobby. _____

2. She learned the method from her grandmother in the Ukraine. _____

3. I will explain the process to you. _____

4. Poke a tiny hole in each end of a raw egg. _____

5. Blow gently into one of the holes. _____

6. The egg yolk drips out of the other hole. _____

7. Paint designs on the egg with melted wax. _____

8. Soak the egg in bright dye. _____

9. The dye colors only the unwaxed parts of the egg. _____

10. Ukrainians call these eggs *pysanky*. _____

G.U.M.

Extra Practice

Lesson 3 Each sentence has a compound subject or a compound predicate. Circle the two or three simple subjects that make up each compound subject. Underline the two verbs that make up each compound predicate.

1. Katie and Varsha went on a backpacking trip.

2. Squirrels, chipmunks, and lizards scampered across the trail.

3. They hiked to the campground and selected a campsite.

4. Varsha set up the tent and rolled out the sleeping bags.

5. Katie gathered wood and made dinner.

6. Wind and rain fell all night.

7. Katie and Varsha aired their gear in the morning sun.

8. The sunshine and crisp air were refreshing.

9. The campers caught a trout and cooked it for breakfast.

10. They packed up and hiked home in the afternoon.

Lesson 4 Circle each direct object in the sentences below. Underline the indirect object. Not every sentence has an indirect object.

1. Last weekend we gave our dog a present.

2. We made him a new doghouse.

3. My mother bought scrap wood and shingles at a lumberyard.

4. A library book gave us ideas for the design.

5. My father sawed the wood to the right length.

6. My little brother handed me the nails.

7. I hammered them carefully into the wood.

8. The dog watched us curiously.

9. Finally, we finished the house.

10. The dog wagged his tail.

Name _____

Lesson 5 Write *PN* if the boldfaced word is a predicate noun. Write *PA* if the boldfaced word is a predicate adjective. Circle the linking verb in each sentence.

1. Garlic is an **herb**. ____

2. It is **popular** in many kinds of cooking. ____

3. Garlic is a white **bulb**. ____

4. Its outer skin feels **dry**. ____

5. Garlic is a healthful **food**. ____

6. It is **good** for people with high blood pressure. ____

7. The odor of garlic is **strong**. ____

8. Garlic smells **bad**, according to some people. ____

9. However, it tastes **delicious**. ____

10. Garlic is my favorite **seasoning**. ____

Lesson 6 Underline each prepositional phrase. Circle the preposition that begins each phrase. Draw a box around the object of the preposition. There may be more than one prepositional phrase in each sentence.

1. Ralph and I rented roller skates at the harbor.

2. Skating was hard at first.

3. One foot rolled to the left, and one rolled to the right.

4. I fell on the ground again and again.

5. Skating became easier after a while.

6. We zoomed along the walkway.

7. We swooped around a streetlight.

8. We skated along the boardwalk.

9. Ralph and I skated for hours.

10. We'll go skating again on the weekend.

Extra Practice

Lesson 7 Write *A* if the verb in the sentence is in the active voice. Write *P* if the verb is in the passive voice.

1. My class held a talent show last week. ___

2. Fliers were made by a class committee. ___

3. Invitations were sent by our teacher to all parents. ___

4. We set up chairs in the gym. ___

5. Two students danced a clog dance. ___

6. A song was sung by my friend Reiko. ___

7. Keith and I performed magic tricks. ___

8. Everyone was astonished by our disappearing pineapple. ___

9. Jokes were told by Jamal. ___

10. The show was enjoyed by all. ___

Lesson 8 Underline the appositive phrase in each sentence.

1. Eohippus, the prehistoric ancestor of modern horses, was less than two feet tall.

2. Artifacts found at Susa, an ancient city in Asia, show that people rode horses 5,000 years ago.

3. The Arabian, a strong breed of horse, was developed in the Middle East for desert riding.

4. Breeders developed thoroughbreds, swift and powerful racehorses, from Arabian horses.

5. The quarter horse, the favorite breed of most American cattle ranchers, is fast and sure-footed.

6. The shire, the largest of all horse breeds, is descended from the heavy war horses that once carried knights into battle.

7. The Shetland pony, one of the smallest of all horse breeds, can be less than three feet tall.

8. The Appaloosa, a breed with small dark spots on its coat, was brought to America by the Spanish and bred by the Nez Perce people.

9. The ancestors of mustangs, wild horses in the western United States, were tame horses that escaped from their owners.

10. Przewalski's horse, an endangered species, is the last of all the wild horse breeds.

Name _____

Lesson 9 Write *CD* next to each compound sentence and *CX* next to each complex sentence.

1. When the weekend weather is good, I usually ride my bike through my neighborhood. ___

2. If I pass a friend, I say hello. ___

3. Although I have biked here many times, I always see something new. ___

4. There may be a street fair, or someone may have planted a new garden. ___

5. The grocery stores have boxes of fruit outside, and the fruit varies with the season. ___

6. My favorite is the kiwi fruit; it's the kind with fuzzy brown skin and green flesh. ___

7. I often bicycle to Spring Street, although it's a long ride. ___

8. Because the return trip is mostly downhill, it's both fast and fun. ___

9. I don't like riding my bicycle after dark; I go home before sunset. ___

10. Biking is fun on nice days, but it is not so pleasant in rain or snow. ___

Lesson 10 Write *F* after each fragment. Write *RO* after each run-on. Write *CS* after each comma splice. Write *RA* after each ramble-on sentence.

1. The amazing baobab tree. ___

2. The most famous baobabs grow in Africa, they are also found on the island of Madagascar. ___

3. These trees have incredibly thick trunks they may grow up to fifty feet in diameter. ___

4. Because baobabs store water in their trunks. ___

5. On the hot, dry plains where baobabs live it is not very moist, and water is precious to the thirsty inhabitants of this parched environment. ___

6. The white flowers of the baobab open only at night, bats pollinate them. ___

7. The tree's fruit is called "monkey bread" it grows almost a foot long. ___

8. Dangles from a long stem. ___

9. People eat baobab fruit, they use the leaves and bark in medicines. ___

10. Although the bark is most often used for paper, cloth, and rope. ___

Extra Practice

Lesson 11 Underline the word in parentheses that best identifies each boldfaced noun.

1. Leonard Nimoy played the **part** of Mr. Spock on *Star Trek*. (common/proper/plural)

2. Maybe this character's name jogged **viewers'** memories of childcare expert Dr. Benjamin Spock. (singular/proper/possessive)

3. **Dr. Spock's** famous handbook is titled *Baby and Child Care.* (common/plural/possessive)

4. My encyclopedia has an entry for Dr. Spock, but none for **Mr. Spock.** (common/proper/possessive)

5. Does your **school's** encyclopedia have an entry for him? (plural/proper/possessive)

6. The first *Star Trek* show was cancelled because **people** weren't watching it. (singular/plural/possessive)

7. *Star Trek* led to *Star Trek: The Next Generation.* (common/proper/possessive)

8. Fans called *Trekkies* read **The Star Trek Encyclopedia.** (common/proper/possessive)

9. No doubt that **encyclopedia** has an entry for Mr. Spock. (common/proper/possessive)

10. I'd love to go to one of the **Trekkies'** costume parties dressed as a Klingon! (common/singular/possessive)

Lesson 12 Circle a pronoun in parentheses to complete each sentence correctly.

1. I had to pinch (myself/herself) to make sure I wasn't dreaming.

2. Sometimes we want something so much that we fool (ourselves/us).

3. Yet there it was, and it was (my/myself) very own!

4. Ask (yourself/you): wouldn't you be thrilled if you got one for *your* birthday?

5. For weeks the three of (us/ourselves) had discussed it. My parents had also talked about it.

6. I was sure they would persuade (themselves/ourselves) not to get one for me.

7. However, my dad had had one (himself/itself) when he wasn't much older than I.

8. And Mom (herself/she) admitted that she had always wanted one.

9. My grandparents had wanted to get her one, but (their/themselves) apartment was small.

10. When my parents drove up in their car last night, I thought I saw a puppy in (its/itself) backseat. I was right!

Lesson 13 Circle each boldfaced interrogative pronoun. Underline each boldfaced indefinite pronoun.

1. "Can I get you **anything** from the Copper Coffee Pot?" asked Max.

2. "**What** are they serving these days?" asked Carmina.

3. "They have ten different kinds of muffins, and **all** are delicious."

4. "Surprise me," said Carmina. "I love **everything** they serve."

5. Then she asked, "**Who** runs that place now? Are Carl and Caroline Andersen still the owners?"

6. "Yes, and **both** still work long days in the kitchen," said Max.

7. "I've seen 60-year-olds who keep fit, but **few** seem as happy and healthy as the Andersens," he added.

8. "Yes," said Carmina, "and **nobody** bakes muffins quite like Mr. Andersen."

9. "**Who** created those recipes?" wondered Carmina.

10. "It must have been **someone** very talented," said Max.

Lesson 14 Circle each action verb. Underline each linking verb.

1. A kangaroo is a mammal with large, powerful hind legs.

2. Like bettongs, potoroos, and wallabies, kangaroos are *macropods*.

3. Both red kangaroos and gray kangaroos live in Australia.

4. *Joey* is the name for a baby kangaroo.

5. A newborn joey is only about an inch long.

6. The joey completes its development in its mother's pouch.

7. A kangaroo hops on its hind legs.

8. Large kangaroos hop as fast as 30 miles per hour for short distances.

9. A kangaroo uses its tail for balance.

10. A red kangaroo's tail may be more than three feet long.

Lesson 15 Circle each boldfaced present-tense verb. Underline each boldfaced past-tense verb. Draw a box around each boldfaced future-tense verb.

1. Last month I **read** a book of Greek myths.

2. I **enjoyed** the myth about King Midas.

3. The god Bacchus **granted** Midas a single wish.

4. He **wished** that everything he touched would turn to gold.

5. I **do** not **think** that this was a smart wish.

6. The king's dinner **turned** into gold as soon as he tried eating it.

7. This myth **teaches** a valuable lesson about impulsiveness and greed.

8. Sometime I **will tell** you another Greek myth.

9. Next month I **will look** for a book of Native American tales.

10. Soon our local library **will have** an even better folktale collection.

Lesson 16 Circle each boldfaced verb in the present perfect tense. Underline each boldfaced verb in the past perfect tense.

1. People in many cultures **have created** stories that explain the origin of things.

2. Anya **has read** some of these stories.

3. She **has told** me one story.

4. The Pemon people of Venezuela **had observed** that vultures eat jaguars' leftovers.

5. For generations, they **have told** a story that explains why.

6. According to the legend, King Vulture **has helped** other animals when they encounter trouble.

7. One time, King Vulture **had helped** a foolish jaguar.

8. Ever since that time, jaguars **have given** food to King Vulture in gratitude.

9. On a trip to the mountains, Anya **had seen** two vultures flying in circles.

10. Since then, she **has wondered** if there was a jaguar nearby.

Name _____

Lesson 17 Circle each boldfaced verb in a progressive tense. Cross out each boldfaced verb that is not in a progressive tense.

1. I **am making** a rug out of old T-shirts.

2. I **have chosen** which colors to include.

3. In a few weeks my family **will be using** this rug as a bathmat.

4. The past few summers I **have helped** my aunt in her craft shop.

5. Hazel Shoemaker **was teaching** a rug-braiding class there two summers ago.

6. I took Hazel's class that summer, and this coming summer I **will be taking** it again.

7. I **have remembered** a beautiful red, green, and blue rug of Hazel's ever since that summer.

8. She **was putting** the finishing touches on it.

9. She **had braided** it out of worn-out wool blankets.

10. Maybe someday I **will be teaching** rug braiding to kids my age.

Lesson 18 Circle each boldfaced word that is an adjective. Put a box around each boldfaced word that is an adverb.

1. A hummingbird has **extremely** flexible shoulder joints.

2. **Each** wing can turn almost 180 degrees.

3. A hummingbird flaps its wings **constantly**.

4. **Some** hummingbirds beat their wings up to seventy times a second.

5. The rapidly moving wings help the bird fly in **all** directions.

6. The bee hummingbird is **two** inches long.

7. It is the **smallest** bird in the world.

8. Even the giant hummingbird is **only** eight inches long.

9. I'm **often** delighted by the sight of a hovering hummingbird.

10. **Then** the beautiful little bird disappears.

Extra Practice

Lesson 19 Underline the prepositional phrase in each sentence. Circle the preposition and draw a box around its object. Draw a star above each interjection.

1. Great! This book has a section on hibernation.

2. Some animals enter a sleeplike state during the winter.

3. Hibernation can protect them from the cold.

4. It can also reduce their need for food.

5. In the fall, most warm-blooded hibernators eat steadily.

6. Wow, some live on their stored fat!

7. Others store food in their burrows.

8. Hey, did you know that hibernating mammals and birds do not sleep through the entire winter?

9. Their "deep hibernation" periods alternate with wakeful periods.

10. Turtles and frogs may hibernate in frozen ponds.

Lesson 20 Underline each coordinating conjunction. Circle each subordinating conjunction.

1. Since I don't like tomatoes, you shouldn't serve spaghetti.

2. Actually, I like tomatoes if they have been cooked.

3. I like tomato juice and catsup, but I don't like tomato salsa.

4. I know you don't like raisins or sunflower seeds.

5. You should take some trail mix before I add them.

6. Although I hate cooked raisins, I love raw ones.

7. Since raisins get soft when they're cooked, I can't stand them in cookies or cinnamon rolls.

8. I detest raw sunflower seeds, but I love them fried in oil.

9. Since you're such a picky eater, maybe you should do the cooking for our picnic.

10. I've been called a gourmet, but I've never been called picky!

Name _____

Lesson 21 Circle the correct word in parentheses.

1. "Isn't (your/you're) math test tomorrow?" asked Ilana.

2. "Yes, and I could use (your/you're) help," Sam replied.

3. "(Your/You're) good at math, aren't you?" he asked.

4. "(Your/You're) right, I am," Ilana answered.

5. "(Your/You're) going to do very well on the test if you study tonight," she assured him.

6. "I wish I shared (your/you're) confidence," Sam sighed.

7. "I'll try to explain the things (your/you're) confused about," she said.

8. "Bring (your/you're) math book over here so we can get started," Ilana continued.

9. "I hope (your/you're) prepared for a long afternoon," Sam told her.

10. "If (your/you're) willing to spend some time working with me, I think I'll do well on that test," he added.

Lesson 22 Write *their, there,* or *they're* to complete each sentence correctly.

1. "We can land our plane in that family's field over _____!" said Bill.

2. "I hope we don't ruin _____ crops," Bill added.

3. "It looks like _____ nearly all harvested, anyway," his navigator said.

4. "Look up _____!" cried the farmer.

5. "Those people are going to try to land _____ plane on our farm!" his wife said.

6. "Let's call the newspaper. _____ going to love this story," said the farmer.

7. "Try to land _____, on the open field," suggested Bill's navigator.

8. "I see some people. _____ running over to meet us," Bill said.

9. "_____ carrying cameras, too," said his navigator.

10. "It looks like the family called _____ friends!" Bill said.

Name _____

Lesson 23 Write *its* or *it's* to complete each sentence correctly. Remember to capitalize the first word in a sentence.

1. _____ a good night to look at the sky.

2. That comet is now as close to Earth as _____ ever going to be.

3. _____ tail is visible through these binoculars.

4. It will only be visible for a few nights as it moves on _____ path through the sky.

5. _____ possible to see several of the constellations tonight.

6. _____ interesting to read the stories that various cultures have created about the stars.

7. _____ easy to see the bright North Star.

8. Do you know any of _____ other names?

9. To the Navajo, _____ known as The Star That Does Not Move.

10. _____ position in the sky is the same every night, and other stars revolve around it.

Lesson 24 Write *C* after each sentence that is written correctly. Circle each incorrect usage of *go* and *like*.

1. Marika said, "Roberto asked me to help him with his science project." _____

2. Then she went, "I'm not sure if I want to, though." _____

3. I was like, "I thought you admired his science project." _____

4. "Last week you were like, he's so smart," I told her. _____

5. Marika said, "He is smart." _____

6. Then she goes, "But I don't like his project as much as I thought I did." _____

7. I go, "What's wrong with it?" _____

8. She was like, "There's nothing really wrong with it." _____

9. "It's just that I'm not sure it has a chance to win an award in the science fair competition," she admitted. _____

10. "I think I'd like to do a project on my own," she said. _____

Lesson 25 Circle the correct word in parentheses.

1. "This is a (good/well) place for our secret clubhouse," said Josie.

2. "It's (good/well) hidden here in the woods."

3. "Yes," said Carrie, "let's start building it while the weather is still (good/well)."

4. Josie replied, "Okay, but I also want to plan it (good/well)."

5. Then she said, "Carrie, how (good/well) can you use a saw?"

6. "Those branches will make (good/well) walls," she continued.

7. "Yes, but what can we use for a roof that will keep the rain out (good/well)?" asked Carrie.

8. "I think that old umbrella would make a (good/well) roof."

9. "What a (good/well) idea!" exclaimed Josie.

10. Carrie smiled and said, "Our clubhouse will be a (good/well) place to invite our friends."

Lesson 26 Write *doesn't* or *don't* to complete each sentence correctly.

1. I _____ know what to serve at my birthday party next week.

2. What one person likes, another person _____ like.

3. It would be fun to make pot stickers, but Ana _____ like them.

4. I love nachos with hot salsa, but Vivian and Raoul _____ like spicy food.

5. My mom asked, "Why _____ you have a fondue party?"

6. That's a good idea, but we _____ have enough forks for dipping.

7. Of course, I'll have a cake, but I _____ know what flavor to get.

8. Jeremy, Sandra, and Paco like chocolate, but Deborah _____.

9. Finally, Dad asked, "Why _____ you just have a potluck?"

10. If everyone brings a dish he or she likes, I _____ think anyone will leave hungry.

Name _____

Extra Practice

Lesson 27 Write *whose* or *who's* to complete each sentence correctly. Remember to capitalize the first word in a sentence.

1. _____ ready to go on the picnic?

2. _____ bringing the tuna sandwiches?

3. Bonnie knows _____ turn it is to bring the drinks.

4. Carlos should know _____ coming.

5. _____ sweatshirt is this?

6. Did somebody figure out _____ going to bring the games?

7. Luke can't remember _____ Frisbee he brought.

8. It belongs to the person _____ name is written on it.

9. _____ ice cream is melting on the blanket?

10. I wonder _____ going to clean up.

Lesson 28 Write *to, too,* or *two* to complete each sentence correctly.

1. The _____ soccer teams are taking their places on the field.

2. The team that wins this game will advance _____ the championship match.

3. The players are very excited, and the spectators are, _____.

4. The _____ center forwards face each other for the kickoff.

5. Our left wing has moved _____ an open area.

6. Our center forward passes the ball _____ her, and she dribbles toward the goal.

7. After _____ periods, the match is still scoreless.

8. The game will be decided by a shootout; each team must choose five players

   _____ participate as shooters.

9. Our first _____ shooters score goals!

10. The final score is four _____ three in favor of our team!

Name _____

Lesson 29 Circle the correct word in parentheses.

1. (Leave/Let) me tell you about my favorite activities.

2. To throw a Frisbee, (raise/rise) your arm to shoulder level.

3. Draw your hand back, and then (leave/let) the Frisbee go.

4. Once you master the yo-yo, it will (raise/rise) and fall at your command.

5. The wind helps (raise/rise) a kite into the air.

6. If there is no wind, you may need to run to get it to (raise/rise).

7. If you (leave/let) your ice skates out in the rain, the leather may be ruined.

8. My community is trying to (raise/rise) money to build a playground.

9. Right now we have to (leave/let) our neighborhood to play many of these games.

10. My parents never (leave/let) me play in the street.

Lesson 30 Circle the correct word in parentheses.

1. In 1930, Fred P. Newton (swam/swum) 1,826 miles down the Mississippi River.

2. No one has (swam/swum) as far since then.

3. Hilary Walker (ran/runned) 590 miles, from Lhasa, Tibet, to Kathmandu, Nepal.

4. After 14 days, she had (ran/run) the entire length of the Friendship Highway.

5. Pilot John Edward Long has (flew/flown) 59,300 hours since he began flying in 1933.

6. Lyle Shelton won the 1991 National Championship Air Race, in which he (flew/flied) at an average speed of 481.618 miles per hour.

7. Wang Junxia of Beijing, China, set women's records for 3,000 and 10,000 meters when she (ran/runned) in races in 1993.

8. The first person who (flew/flied) faster than the speed of sound was Chuck Yeager.

9. Kenya's Paul Ereng set a world record in 1989 when he (ran/runned) 800 meters in 1 minute, 44.84 seconds in 1989.

10. Aleksandr Popov and Matt Biondi are the only people who have (swam/swum) the 100-meter freestyle in less than 49 seconds.

Extra Practice

Lesson 31 Circle each boldfaced word that is a subject pronoun. Underline each boldfaced word that is an object pronoun.

1. Last Saturday Kiko showed **me** how to make a kite.

2. **She** learned how to do this from an older cousin.

3. First **you** take one wooden dowel and glue **it** across another.

4. Then **you** take colorful paper and cut **it** in a diamond shape.

5. **You** attach the paper to the frame carefully but firmly.

6. To make a tail, **you** take strings of crepe paper and glue **them** to the back corner of the kite.

7. Finally, **you** get a long string and attach **it** to the frame with a special knot.

8. When Kiko and **I** finished these steps, **we** took our kites to the park.

9. The wind was just right, and **it** lifted **them** into the air.

10. Some people admired our kites and asked **us** how **we** made **them**.

Lesson 32 Circle the correct pronoun in each pair.

1. Mr. Merrick promised Shari, Deepak, and (me/I) a ride in his hot-air balloon.

2. When the big day finally arrived, Shari and (he/him) arrived at my house early in the morning.

3. When we got to the field, (he/him) and Mariel were already there.

4. They asked Deepak and (she/her) for help in unfolding the huge, colorful balloon.

5. Mr. Merrick told Mariel and (me/I) to turn the basket on its side and attach it to the bottom of the balloon.

6. He warned Shari and (us/we) to stand back while he lit the burner.

7. (We/Us) and Mr. Merrick watched the balloon fill with hot air.

8. When the balloon stood upright, (they/them) and Mr. Merrick climbed into the basket.

9. Mariel and (me/I) watched them slowly rise into the air.

10. Next time, (he/him) and I will ride in the balloon.

Name _____

Lesson 33 Circle the antecedent of each boldfaced pronoun.

1. Last summer Naleema visited her relatives in India. **They** live in Bombay.

2. Naleema was excited about the trip. **She** had never met her aunts and uncles in India.

3. When Naleema and her parents arrived in Bombay, **they** were tired from the long flight.

4. Luckily, her uncle picked them up at the airport. **He** was so happy to see Naleema that he picked her up and swung her in circles.

5. On the way to his house, he explained that Bombay is sometimes called Bollywood because **it** is home to India's huge movie industry.

6. Naleema didn't meet any movie stars, but she did see some amazing sites. **They** included the Taj Mahal.

7. The Taj Mahal is a beautiful building. **It** is made out of white marble.

8. In the seventeenth century, Shah Jahan ordered it built. **He** wanted to create a beautiful tomb for his wife.

9. About 20,000 workers built the Taj Mahal. It took **them** twenty years.

10. Naleema had a great trip to India, but **it** was too short!

Lesson 34 Circle the correct word in parentheses.

1. I picked up the telephone and said, "Hello, (who/whom) is there?"

2. "This is Mrs. Li. Are you the person (who/whom) entered the cookie contest?"

3. "No," I replied, "that was my mother, (who/whom) bakes the best cookies in the world."

4. "With (who/whom) can I discuss her entry?" asked Mrs. Li.

5. "I can help you," I said excitedly. "(Who/Whom) won the contest?"

6. "Of the hundreds of people (who/whom) competed, your mother entered the best recipe."

7. "Let me add that the judges were cookie experts for (who/whom) cookie tasting is an art."

8. I responded proudly, "I am the person on (who/whom) she tested each recipe to find the winning cookie."

9. "Well," said Mrs. Li, "you are obviously a young man (who/whom) knows your cookies."

10. I can't wait to tell my mother (who/whom) called while she was out.

Name _____

Extra Practice

Lesson 35 Underline the correct form of each verb in parentheses.

1. Many types of vegetables (grow/grows) in my uncle's garden.

2. Green bean vines (climb/climbs) up the back fence.

3. Two varieties of squash (thrive/thrives) in the corner.

4. Three rows of corn (grow/grows) as tall as my uncle.

5. Sometimes they (make/makes) a good hiding place when we play hide-and-seek.

6. Five big watermelons (rest/rests) on the ground.

7. A patch of wildflowers (brighten/brightens) the whole garden.

8. Shiny purple eggplants (glisten/glistens) in the sunlight.

9. Round heads of cabbage (grow/grows) next to the tomatoes.

10. Vegetables from the garden (taste/tastes) terrific!

Lesson 36 Underline the correct form of *be* in each sentence.

1. I (am/are) so excited about visiting Grandma Esther in Georgia.

2. My family visits her every summer when school (is/are) finished.

3. During my last visit, there (was/were) a quilting bee at her house.

4. Grandma Esther's friends (was/were) at the bee.

5. They (was/were) all happy to see me and show me their quilts.

6. I (was/were) invited to drink lemonade and to watch the women quilt.

7. Grandma pointed to a yellow square that (was/were) at the center of her quilt.

8. She told me that it (was/were) from a dress that my mother wore when she was my age.

9. It (is/are) interesting to think about how long Grandma saved that dress.

10. This year, I (am/are) bringing scraps of material so I can start my own quilt.

Name _____

Lesson 37 Underline the form of the verb that gives the correct sense of time.

1. Rashad (is/has been) at work on that painting for three months.

2. He (buys/bought) the canvas, paints, and brushes last October.

3. He (chose/chooses) a beautiful forest scene to paint.

4. He (hoped/hopes) to finish the painting next week.

5. After he finishes, he (enters/will enter) the painting in the annual art contest.

6. Each year the judges (award/had awarded) a blue ribbon to the best painting.

7. The winner of this year's blue ribbon (had received/will receive) a set of oil paints.

8. All of the paintings (will appear/had appeared) in the art exhibit that will follow.

9. Last year Monique (wins/won) the blue ribbon.

10. Since then, Rashad (becomes/has become) a much better painter.

Lesson 38 Circle a verb in parentheses to complete each sentence correctly.

1. You and Jerry (is/are) late for the picnic.

2. The #63 bus or #57 bus (take/takes) passengers right to the entrance of the park.

3. You and Margaret (make/makes) the best fried chicken.

4. The petting zoo and the merry-go-round (stay/stays) open late during the summer.

5. Margaret and Shauna (like/likes) to pet the llamas at the zoo.

6. Sometimes the zookeeper or the animal trainer (show/shows) visitors around the monkey house.

7. A big pretzel or a fruit bar (taste/tastes) great.

8. The big oak tree or the entrance gate (is/are) a good place to meet afterward.

9. Victor or Cheema (has/have) the keys to the car.

10. Don't forget that Jerry and Cheema (need/needs) to be home by six o'clock.

Lesson 39 Underline the correct form of the adjective in parentheses.

1. Last night Lisa's basketball team played the (better/best) game they have played all season.

2. They trained (harder/hardest) than they did last year.

3. Several key players are much (taller/tallest) than they were last year.

4. Lisa jumps (higher/highest) than anyone else on the team.

5. She hopes to be named the team's (more valuable/most valuable) player.

6. But the team is at its (better/best) when everyone works together.

7. The players move (faster/fastest) than lightning up and down the court.

8. When Lisa made a basket, her family cheered (louder/loudest) than anyone else.

9. The game was the (closer/closest) one I've seen this year.

10. Lisa's team played (better/best) than their opponents, and they came away with a one-point victory.

Lesson 40 Write an auxiliary verb to complete each sentence. There is more than one way to complete some sentences.

1. We _____ arrive at the beach in about ten minutes.

2. The forecast predicts sunshine this morning, but it _____ rain during the afternoon.

3. There _____ be a storm out at sea.

4. I wonder if we _____ plan on leaving early.

5. Maybe we _____ just stay until it starts getting cloudy.

6. It _____ stay sunny after all.

7. It _____ not rain at all.

8. I guess we _____ stop and buy sandwiches on the way to the beach.

9. I hope the ocean _____ be warm enough to swim in.

10. I wish we _____ go to the beach more often.

Name _____

Lesson 41 Cross out incorrect punctuation and add correct punctuation. Draw three lines (≡) under each lowercase letter that should be capitalized. Then label each sentence *declarative, interrogative, imperative,* or *exclamatory.*

1. what is the oldest form of footwear. _____

2. the first shoe ever made was the sandal? _____

3. The Greeks wore decorated sandals called *krepis* _____

4. look at this photograph. _____

5. it shows a sandal found in an Egyptian tomb? _____

6. What is it made of. _____

7. read the caption below the picture _____

8. It says the sandal was made of papyrus? _____

9. Wasn't papyrus also used for paper. _____

10. yes, the ancient Egyptians were quite resourceful. _____

Lesson 42 Draw three lines (≡) under each lowercase letter that should be capitalized. Draw a line (/) through each capital letter that should be lowercase.

1. My friend julia did research to learn about the History of fans.

2. fans were first used in egypt and china more than 5,000 years Ago.

3. In the hot egyptian climate, Cooling breezes were welcome.

4. Huge fans made of woven Papyrus cooled royal rulers such as nefertiti and tutankhamun.

5. Ancient chinese fans Were made of peacock feathers.

6. The chinese introduced the fan to the japanese, who invented the Folding Fan.

7. Have you ever Visited the cherry blossom fan shop on becker street?

8. It is owned by mrs. tanaka and her Husband.

9. They import fans from japan, china, and Korea.

10. In july and august the Demand for fans increases.

Extra Practice

Lesson 43 Rewrite each item below. Use initials and abbreviations where you can.

1. Mister Everett Rhodes Castle _____

2. Mistress Madeline Ross _____

3. 4232 Avalon Boulevard _____

4. Doctor Paul Minetti _____

5. 285 Hyde Street _____

6. November 9, 1997 _____

7. February 12, 1997 _____

8. Monday, September 19 _____

9. Techno Corporation _____

10. Mister Juan Herrera _____

Lesson 44 Circle the letters that should be capitalized. Underline and add quotation marks where they are needed in titles.

1. I saw a movie documentary titled Ancient ways.

2. It was based on the book america's ancestors.

3. My class read the poem hiawatha.

4. Then we wrote a class poem titled the river is calling.

5. Have you seen the movie rain chasers?

6. Its theme song is titled rain dance.

7. My favorite song is eagle flight.

8. My aunt gave me the book coyote tales.

9. My favorite story is called coyote steals the stars.

10. I also enjoyed the story how the turtle got its tail.

Name _____

Lesson 45 Underline the correct word in parentheses. If the word is a possessive, write *possessive.* If the word is a contraction, write the two words it was made from.

1. My (sisters/sister's) favorite story is "Cinderella." _____

2. Have you ever wondered about this (stories/story's) history? _____

3. Historians (don't/dont') know exactly when and where the first version was told. _____

4. (It's/Its) probable that the story originated in China. _____

5. The Chinese (versions/version's) main character is called Yeh-Hsien. _____

6. Yeh-Hsien attends a festival, with a magic (fish's/fishes) help. _____

7. The Chinese Cinderella story was first recorded in the ninth century by one of the (worlds/world's) first collectors of folktales. _____

8. A person named Charles Perrault collected a French (storyteller's/storytellers') version of the Cinderella story. _____

9. These (aren't/are'nt) the only two versions of this story. _____

10. (You'll/Youl'l) be surprised to learn that more than 700 versions of the Cinderella story have been collected. _____

Lesson 46 Add commas where they belong. Circle commas that don't belong. Remember that a comma is not needed to separate two items in a series.

1. Children have played with marbles tops and board games for thousands of years.

2. Simple marbles were made of stones animal bones, and balls of clay.

3. Inhabitants of England, and Ireland used marbles made of chestnuts hazelnuts and, olives.

4. Semiprecious stones such as agate, and jasper were used as marbles in ancient Greece.

5. Historians believe that marble games were played in, Egypt Europe and equatorial Africa.

6. A board game called *senet* was played by children adults and pharaohs in ancient Egypt.

7. A senet game board, and game pieces were found in King Tutankhamun's tomb.

8. Game pieces were usually made of ivory, and stone.

9. Chess checkers and senet are some of the world's oldest games.

10. Greeks Romans and Egyptians all played different variations of checkers.

Name _____

Extra Practice

Lesson 47 Add the missing comma to each sentence. Then decide why the comma is needed. Write *I* for introductory word, *C* for compound sentence, and *D* for direct address.

1. "Mr. Moss can you tell me how this vase was made?" Claudia asked. _____

2. "Well it began as a lump of clay," Mr. Moss said. _____

3. "The potter pounded the clay and then she placed an even mound in the center of a potter's wheel," he went on. _____

4. "She turned the wheel with her foot and she molded the spinning clay into this shape," he explained. _____

5. "Is that the only way vases are made Mr. Moss?" Deshaun asked. _____

6. "No different potters use different methods," he answered. _____

7. "Some potters roll clay into long coils and they use the coils to shape pots," Claudia said. _____

8. "Claudia is it true that all pots must be fired in a kiln?" Deshaun asked. _____

9. "Yes the intense heat strengthens the clay," Claudia answered. _____

10. "The potter glazed this pot with paint and then she fired it a second time," Mr. Moss explained. _____

Lesson 48 Write a semicolon or a colon to separate the independent clauses in each sentence. Sentences 3, 5, and 9 require a colon.

1. My uncle is a deep sea diver he searches for shipwrecks in the Caribbean.

2. His crew discovered a sunken ship last year it was more than 300 years old.

3. The crew knew exactly what to do they contacted a local archaeological society.

4. Archaeologists helped them recover the ship's cargo the divers worked very carefully.

5. Many unusual items were found coins, iron swords, and eating utensils were among them.

6. The Caribbean was not safe in the 1600s many ships were captured by pirates.

7. Some ships were lost in storms others sank as a result of battles.

8. Many shipwrecks rest on the ocean floor they are difficult to locate.

9. My uncle has learned one thing patience and persistence are important.

10. Someday I hope to become a diver sunken ships fascinate me.

Lesson 49 Write *I* after each indirect quotation and *D* after each direct quotation. Then add quotation marks and other punctuation to the direct quotations. Draw three lines (≡) under each lowercase letter that should be capitalized.

1. How is glass made? Tony asked. _____

2. Mrs. Woo explained that glass is made from a mixture of sand, ash, and limestone. _____

3. These ingredients are melted together in a furnace, she explained. _____

4. She said, the ingredients combine to form a thick syrup, which hardens into glass. _____

5. It can also be spun into fibers to make fiberglass, she said. _____

6. Mrs. Woo explained that glass is one of the most useful substances on Earth. _____

7. When was glass invented? Tony asked _____

8. Historians believe that Egyptians first made glass 3,500 years ago, Mrs. Woo said. _____

9. She explained that long ago only the very rich owned objects made of glass. _____

10. Ancient peoples considered glass as valuable as jewels she said. _____

Lesson 50 Rewrite this business letter in correct letter form on the blanks.

The Insect Zoo 4334 W. Peachtree Drive Atlanta, Georgia 30301 October 22, 1997 Dear Sir or Madam: I am writing a report about carnivorous plants. Please send me information about the Venus's-flytrap. Sincerely, Leon S. Berstein 203 Birch Street Augusta, Georgia 30903

_____

_____

_____

_____

_____

_____

_____

_____

_____

_____

_____

G.U.M.

Choose the answer that describes the underlined part of each sentence. Fill in the circle next to your answer.

1. Paul Newman <u>played a Wild West outlaw in</u> *Butch Cassidy and the Sundance Kid*.
   - (a) complete subject
   - (b) complete predicate

2. <u>This famous actor</u> is very honorable in real life, however.
   - (a) complete subject
   - (b) simple subject

3. Newman <u>makes</u> his own brand of salad dressing.
   - (a) complete predicate
   - (b) simple predicate

4. <u>The profits from the salad dressing</u> go to charity.
   - (a) complete predicate
   - (b) complete subject

5. <u>Movies</u> and <u>salad dressings</u> are not Newman's only interests.
   - (a) compound subject
   - (b) compound predicate

6. He <u>owns</u> sports cars and <u>races</u> them.
   - (a) compound subject
   - (b) compound predicate

7. Jodie Foster became <u>famous</u> at a very young age.
   - (a) direct object
   - (b) predicate adjective

8. She played leading <u>roles</u> in several Disney adventures.
   - (a) direct object
   - (b) indirect object

9. As an adult, Foster became an excellent <u>actor</u>.
   - (a) predicate noun
   - (b) predicate adjective

10. Foster's acting talent has brought <u>her</u> two Academy Awards.
    - (a) direct object
    - (b) indirect object

11. Foster is also a respected <u>director</u>.
    - (a) predicate noun
    - (b) direct object

12. She directed <u>*Little Man Tate*</u>, the story of a child genius.
    - (a) predicate adjective
    - (b) direct object

13. African American actors have had difficulty getting good roles <u>in Hollywood movies</u>.
    - (a) appositive
    - (b) prepositional phrase

14. Morgan Freeman, <u>a famous African American actor</u>, has played important roles in several major films.
    - (a) appositive
    - (b) prepositional phrase

15. Freeman moved to Hollywood <u>from New York</u>.
    - (a) appositive
    - (b) prepositional phrase

Name _____

Decide which word is the simple subject of each sentence. Fill in the circle that matches your answer.

16. Some actors in Hollywood become world famous.

    (a) actors   (b) Hollywood   (c) understood *you*

17. Tell me about your favorite movie star.

    (a) Tell   (b) star   (c) understood *you*

Read each sentence and decide which phrase correctly describes it. Fill in the circle next to your answer.

18. Audiences have made Tom Hanks one of Hollywood's most popular actors.

    (a) active voice   (b) passive voice

19. Leading roles are often offered first to Hanks by directors.

    (a) active voice   (b) passive voice

20. He has been compared by critics to such great leading men of Hollywood's Golden Era as James Stewart and Gary Cooper.

    (a) active voice   (b) passive voice

21. Hanks's first leading role was in *Splash*, but his role in *Big* made him a star.

    (a) compound sentence   (b) complex sentence

22. In *Splash* Hanks rescues a mermaid; in *Big* he plays a child in an adult's body.

    (a) compound sentence   (b) complex sentence

23. Because Hanks almost always plays kind characters, audiences see him as a nice man.

    (a) compound sentence   (b) complex sentence

24. Hanks played an unusual character in *Forrest Gump*, that movie made a huge amount of money.

    (a) comma splice   (b) compound sentence

25. Although *E.T.* made the most money of all.

    (a) run-on   (b) fragment

26. Movies that make a lot of money for the studio that produced them are often called *money-makers* because of their proven ability to make large amounts of money.

    (a) fragment   (b) ramble-on

27. Tom Hanks's movies attract large audiences he is a talented actor.

    (a) run-on   (b) ramble-on

28. Two Academy Awards for Best Actor.

    (a) fragment   (b) comma splice

Decide which kind of noun each boldfaced word is. There is only one correct answer to each question. Fill in the circle next to your answer.

1. There may be active **volcanoes** on Venus.
   (a) plural   (b) singular   (c) possessive

2. In 1991 the *Magellan,* a spacecraft, took photos of Venus.
   (a) plural   (b) common   (c) proper

3. It photographed a mountain **peak** on Venus.
   (a) plural   (b) singular   (c) proper

4. It appeared that the **mountain's** sides were covered with lava.
   (a) plural   (b) proper   (c) possessive

Decide which phrase correctly describes the boldfaced verb. Fill in the circle next to your answer.

5. Mercury **is** the planet closest to the sun.
   (a) action verb   (b) linking verb

6. Mercury's temperatures sometimes **rise** to 1300° F.
   (a) action verb   (b) linking verb

Choose the verb or verb phrase in the correct tense to fit in each sentence. Fill in the circle next to your answer.

7. Today I ____ a report on Saturn; when it's finished, I'll play soccer.
   (a) was writing   (b) had written   (c) wrote   (d) am writing

8. Astronomers ____ at Saturn's rings ever since telescopes were invented.
   (a) have marveled   (b) will marvel   (c) marvel   (d) are marveling

9. In 1610 Galileo first ____ Saturn's rings.
   (a) will have observed   (b) observed   (c) observes   (d) will observe

10. Because Galileo ____ through an imperfect telescope, he thought the rings were moons.
    (a) will be gazing   (b) gazes   (c) was gazing   (d) has gazed

11. Today we know that Saturn's colorful rings ____ flat, thin, and wide.
    (a) had been   (b) are being   (c) will be   (d) are

12. Perhaps someday we ____ how they formed.
    (a) will discover   (b) have discovered   (c) discover   (d) were discovering

13. Before *Voyager 1* traveled past Saturn and sent back photos, no one ____ the rings close up.
    (a) sees   (b) had seen   (c) was seeing   (d) has seen

14. No doubt astronomers ____ Saturn's rings for a long time to come.
    (a) were studying   (b) had studied   (c) will be studying   (d) study

Name _____

Choose the pronoun that could replace the boldfaced word or words. Fill in the circle next to your answer.

15. **Which person** would be brave enough to go to Venus?
(a) Who (b) Whose (c) What (d) Whom

16. **Venus's** average temperature is about 900° F.
(a) Our (b) Whose (c) It (d) Its

17. However, **this hot, dry planet** may once have been covered with water.
(a) they (b) it (c) we (d) itself

18. We humans should consider **humans** lucky that our planet has such mild temperatures.
(a) us (b) them (c) itself (d) ourselves

19. Does **a single person** on Earth wish it were hotter or colder here?
(a) everyone (b) anyone (c) nobody (d) few

Is each boldfaced word an adjective or an adverb? Fill in the circle next to your answer.

20. **An** *aurora,* or natural display of light, can be clearly observed only at night.
(a) adjective (b) adverb

21. Auroras can be green, red, or **purple**.
(a) adjective (b) adverb

22. **Electrically** charged particles from the sun cause auroras.
(a) adjective (b) adverb

Decide whether each boldfaced word is a preposition, a coordinating conjunction, a subordinating conjunction, or an interjection. Fill in the circle next to your answer.

23. The Hubble Space Telescope was named **for** astronomer Edwin Hubble.
(a) preposition (b) coordinating conjunction (c) interjection

24. **Wow,** that bus-sized telescope cost 1.5 billion dollars to build and to launch into orbit!
(a) preposition (b) subordinating conjunction (c) interjection

25. **Because** it had a defective mirror, the Hubble did not work properly for a few years.
(a) coordinating conjunction (b) subordinating conjunction (c) interjection

26. The Hubble was in orbit, **so** it was dangerous to repair it.
(a) preposition (b) coordinating conjunction (c) subordinating conjunction

27. Astronauts traveled to the Hubble on the space shuttle *Endeavor* **and** fixed the telescope.
(a) preposition (b) coordinating conjunction (c) subordinating conjunction

28. The Hubble was working again in time to give a clear view of the collision **between** Comet Shoemaker-Levy 9 and Jupiter.
(a) preposition (b) subordinating conjunction (c) interjection

Decide which word completes each sentence correctly. Fill in the circle next to your answer.

1. ___ brother invited me to go to the Insect Zoo on Saturday.
   - ⓐ Your
   - ⓑ You're

2. I hope ___ going to come with us.
   - ⓐ your
   - ⓑ you're

3. An interesting collection of insects has been gathered by the zookeepers who work ___.
   - ⓐ their
   - ⓑ they're
   - ⓒ there

4. ___ particularly proud of the rhinoceros beetle.
   - ⓐ Their
   - ⓑ They're
   - ⓒ There

5. This beetle is one of the highlights of ___ collection.
   - ⓐ their
   - ⓑ they're
   - ⓒ there

6. This amazing insect can support a weight 850 times heavier than ___ own body weight.
   - ⓐ it's
   - ⓑ its

7. Because of this, ___ considered the strongest creature on Earth.
   - ⓐ it's
   - ⓑ its

8. The zoo has a pair of Goliath beetles, ___.
   - ⓐ too
   - ⓑ to
   - ⓒ two

9. Male Goliath beetles can weigh up ___ 3.5 ounces, making them the heaviest living insects.
   - ⓐ too
   - ⓑ to
   - ⓒ two

10. The ___ Goliath beetles at the zoo only weigh about 2.5 ounces each, however.
    - ⓐ too
    - ⓑ to
    - ⓒ two

11. ___ ready to go to the zoo?
    - ⓐ Who's
    - ⓑ Whose

12. ___ parents are going to drive us?
    - ⓐ Who's
    - ⓑ Whose

Does each sentence use *like* or a form of *go* correctly? Fill in the circle next to your answer.

13. Janelle went, "Did you know that a monarch butterfly holds the world record among butterflies and moths for the longest migration?"
    - ⓐ correct
    - ⓑ incorrect

14. "I would like to know more about that," I answered.
    - ⓐ correct
    - ⓑ incorrect

15. I was like, "Wow! That's a long way to fly!"
    - ⓐ correct
    - ⓑ incorrect

Decide which answer will complete each sentence correctly. Fill in the circle next to your answer.

16. I ___ think my dog has any more fleas.
   (a) doesn't   (b) don't

17. He ___ scratch as much as he used to.
   (a) doesn't   (b) don't

18. The flea powder I used must have worked ___.
   (a) good   (b) well

19. It is a ___ thing the fleas didn't jump on me!
   (a) good   (b) well

20. I hope my parents ___ me start an ant farm.
   (a) leave   (b) let

21. The problem is that they don't want to take care of the ants when I ___ for summer camp.
   (a) leave   (b) let

22. I want to see how the ants ___ their young.
   (a) rise   (b) raise

23. I'm also curious about how ants react when the temperature ___ on sunny days.
   (a) rises   (b) raises

Decide which form of the verb will complete each sentence correctly. Fill in the circle next to your answer.

24. Tropical cockroaches ___ faster than any other insect in the world.
   (a) ran   (b) run   (c) runned

25. In 1991 the world record was set by a cockroach that ___ 3.36 miles per hour, or 50 body lengths per second.
   (a) ran   (b) run   (c) runned

26. The fastest flying insect is an Australian dragonfly that has ___ at speeds up to 36 miles per hour.
   (a) flied   (b) flew   (c) flown

27. In recent experiments, several other insects ___ at the speed of 24 miles per hour.
   (a) flied   (b) flew   (c) flown

28. I saw a lot of insects in the water when I ___ in a pond last week.
   (a) swimmed   (b) swum   (c) swam

29. I don't know any insect that has ___ fast enough to set a world record.
   (a) swimmed   (b) swum   (c) swam

Choose the correct pronoun to replace each boldfaced word or phrase. Fill in the circle next to your answer.

1. **Shelley** watched the Grammy Awards ceremony on television.
   - (a) It
   - (b) She
   - (c) We
   - (d) Her

2. **Outstanding musicians** receive this award.
   - (a) Him
   - (b) She
   - (c) He
   - (d) They

3. Shelley told **Maxine** that she wants to be a jazz pianist one day.
   - (a) her
   - (b) it
   - (c) them
   - (d) she

4. **Mr. Sherman** gives Shelley a piano lesson every Tuesday.
   - (a) Him
   - (b) He
   - (c) You
   - (d) It

5. Shelley and **Mr. Sherman** think that Duke Ellington was a musical genius.
   - (a) him
   - (b) he
   - (c) them
   - (d) they

6. Mr. Sherman told Shelley and **Rose** that Ellington began playing piano when he was seven years old.
   - (a) her
   - (b) them
   - (c) she
   - (d) they

Which phrase replaces the boldfaced word in each sentence? Fill in the circle next to your answer.

7. Ellington and his band played at Harlem's legendary Cotton Club; **they** became recognized as some of the nation's best jazz musicians.
   - (a) Ellington
   - (b) his band
   - (c) Ellington and his band

8. Shelley knows a lot about awards given for artistic achievement; I asked **her** to tell me about some of them.
   - (a) Shelley
   - (b) me
   - (c) awards

9. Television producers and performers have their own awards; **they** receive Emmy Awards.
   - (a) performers
   - (b) Television producers and performers
   - (c) Emmy Awards

Choose *who* or *whom* to complete each sentence correctly. Fill in the circle next to your answer.

10. Journalists and writers ___ do excellent work may receive a Pulitzer Prize.
   - (a) who
   - (b) whom

11. To ___ do you think a Pulitzer will be awarded next year?
   - (a) who
   - (b) whom

Which sentence in each pair uses auxiliary verbs correctly? Fill in the circle next to your answer.

12. (a) Akbar would love to meet his favorite hockey player.

   (b) Akbar was love to meet his favorite hockey player.

13. (a) I told Akbar he should write him a letter.

   (b) I told Akbar he had write him a letter.

Name _____

Choose the word or phrase that completes each sentence correctly. Fill in the circle next to your answer.

14. In the eighteenth century, John Newbery ___ the first person to publish books written for children.
    - (a) became
    - (b) becomes

15. Today hundreds of children's books ___ every year.
    - (a) were published
    - (b) are published

16. The Newbery Medal ___ to the author of the best children's book in the United States.
    - (a) is given
    - (b) are given

17. Last year, I ___ *A Wrinkle in Time*.
    - (a) read
    - (b) will read

18. The author, Madeline L'Engle, ___ the Newbery Award for that book.
    - (a) receives
    - (b) received

19. The Caldecott Medal ___ given to the illustrator of the best children's picture book in the United States.
    - (a) are
    - (b) is

20. Later tonight I ___ put my little sister to bed.
    - (a) helped
    - (b) will help

21. She ___ picture books at bedtime.
    - (a) enjoy
    - (b) enjoys

22. Either my mother or my father ___ a book to her every night.
    - (a) read
    - (b) reads

23. Fairy tales and fables ___ her to sleep quickly.
    - (a) put
    - (b) puts

24. Her favorite book ___ *The Polar Express*.
    - (a) is
    - (b) are

25. Its illustrator, Chris Van Allsburg, ___ the Caldecott Medal in 1986.
    - (a) wins
    - (b) won

26. The medal is one of the ___ types of awards.
    - (a) older
    - (b) oldest

27. The ancient Greeks gave gold buttons to their ___ athletes.
    - (a) best
    - (b) most good

28. In any competition a gold medal is ___ to earn than a silver one.
    - (a) more difficult
    - (b) most difficult

Read each sentence and decide whether it is declarative, interrogative, imperative, or exclamatory. Fill in the circle next to your answer.

1. Look at this piece of stone.
   (a) declarative   (b) interrogative   (c) imperative   (d) exclamatory

2. Wow, it's an arrowhead!
   (a) declarative   (b) interrogative   (c) imperative   (d) exclamatory

3. What is it made of?
   (a) declarative   (b) interrogative   (c) imperative   (d) exclamatory

4. It's made of a shiny black rock called *obsidian*.
   (a) declarative   (b) interrogative   (c) imperative   (d) exclamatory

Decide which boldfaced word or words need to be capitalized. Fill in the circle with the letter that matches it.

5. We went **camping** in the **canadian** Rockies.   (a) (b)
       a   b

6. Is it true that dinosaurs once roamed the **state** of **new mexico**?   (a) (b)
            a   b

Choose the correct way to rewrite the boldfaced part of each sentence. Fill in the circle next to your answer.

7. **Doctor Marcus Walter Smith** studies archaeology.
   (a) Dr M. W Smith   (b) Dctr. m w Smith   (c) Dr. M. W. Smith

8. He lives on **Eagen Boulevard**.
   (a) Eag. Blvd.   (b) Eagen blvd.   (c) Eagen Blvd.

9. He works for **Eastmund Corporation**.
   (a) Eastmund Corp.   (b) Eastmund Cp   (c) Eastmund corp.

10. Have you seen the movie **mammoth mania**?
    (a) "Mammoth Mania"   (b) Mammoth Mania   (c) mammoth mania

11. It was based on a short story titled **ice age mysteries**.
    (a) "Ice Age Mysteries"   (b) Ice Age Mysteries   (c) "ice age mysteries"

12. I wrote a poem titled **the Saber tooth cat's revenge**.
    (a) The Saber Tooth Cat's Revenge   (b) "The Saber Tooth Cat's Revenge"

13. Treasure hunters **had not** discovered and destroyed it.
    (a) hadn't   (b) hadnt'   (c) had'nt

14. The **energy of the divers** was fading.
    (a) divers energy   (b) diver's energy   (c) divers' energy

Name _____

G.U.M.

Decide where the comma belongs in each sentence. Fill in the circle with the matching letter.

15. The divers found glass beads, pottery and bronze swords. (a) (b)
    a   b

16. "Did they find jewelry Ms. Anka?" asked Lynette. (a) (b)
    a   b

17. "Yes they found several gold medallions," Ms. Anka answered. (a) (b)
    a   b

18. The divers photographed, sorted and described the objects. (a) (b)
    a b

19. Divers carried the artifacts to the surface but they left them in the water. (a) (b)
    a   b

Which semicolon or colon is needed in each sentence? Fill in the circle next to your answer.

20. The divers were careful: artifacts are: easily damaged. (a) (b)
    a   b

21. The pottery has been underwater for centuries; oxygen would; damage it. (a) (b)
    a   b

22. The vases were kept; in salt water; later, technicians would restore them. (a) (b)
    a   b

23. The divers found gems: rubies and emeralds: were among them. (a) (b)
    a   b

Decide whether each sentence is missing quotation marks or is correct as written. Fill in the circle next to your answer.

24. Where were the artifacts sent next? Lynette asked.
    (a) needs quotation marks   (b) correct as written

25. Ms. Anka explained that they would be sent to a special laboratory for testing.
    (a) needs quotation marks   (b) correct as written

Use the friendly letter below to answer each question. Fill in the circle next to your answer.

26. Which part of the letter is the greeting? (a) (b) (c) (d)

27. Which part of the letter is the body? (a) (b) (c) (d)

a   Camp Mariah
    August 10, 1996

Dear Julio,   b
Camp is great. Yesterday I saw a river otter and an egret.   c

Your buddy,
d   David

Language Handbook Table of Contents

Mechanics

Sentence Structure and Parts of Speech

Usage

Writing a Letter

Guidelines for Listening and Speaking

Name _____

Mechanics

Section 1 Capitalization

- Capitalize the first word in a sentence.
  The kangaroo rat is an amazing animal.

- Capitalize all *proper nouns*, including people's names and the names of particular places.
  Gregory Gordon   Washington Monument

- Capitalize titles of respect.
  Mr. Alvarez   Dr. Chin   Ms. Murphy

- Capitalize family titles used just before people's names and titles of respect that are part of names.
  Uncle Frank   Aunt Mary   Governor Adamson

- Capitalize initials of names.
  Thomas Paul Gerard (T.P. Gerard)

- Capitalize place names.
  France   Utah   China   Baltimore

- Capitalize *proper adjectives,* adjectives that are made from proper nouns.
  Chinese   Icelandic   French   Latin American

- Capitalize the months of the year and the days of the week.
  February   April   Monday   Tuesday

- Capitalize important words in the names of organizations.
  American Lung Association   Veterans of Foreign Wars

- Capitalize important words in the names of holidays.
  Veterans Day   Fourth of July

- Capitalize the first word in the greeting or closing of a letter.
  Dear Edmundo,   Yours truly,

- Capitalize the word *I.*
  Frances and I watched the movie together.

- Capitalize the first, last, and most important words in a title. Be sure to capitalize all verbs including *is* and *was.*
  Island of the Blue Dolphins
  Always Is a Strange Place to Be

- Capitalize the first word in a direct quotation.
  Aunt Rose said, "Please pass the clam dip."

Section 2 Abbreviations and Initials

Abbreviations are shortened forms of words. Many abbreviations begin with a capital letter and end with a period.

- **You can abbreviate titles of address and titles of respect when you write.**
  Mister (Mr. Brian Davis)   Mistress (Mrs. Maria Rosario)
  Doctor (Dr. Emily Chu)   Junior (Everett Castle, Jr.)
  Note: *Ms.* is a title of address used for women. It is not an abbreviation, but it requires a period (Ms. Anita Brown).

- **You can abbreviate words used in addresses when you write.**
  Street (St.)   Avenue (Ave.)   Route (Rte.)   Boulevard (Blvd.)   Road (Rd.)

- **You can abbreviate certain words in the names of businesses when you write.**
  Computers, Incorporated (Computers, Inc.)   Zylar Corporation (Zylar Corp.)

- **You can abbreviate days of the week when you take notes.**
  Sunday (Sun.)   Wednesday (Wed.)   Friday (Fri.)
  Monday (Mon.)   Thursday (Thurs.)   Saturday (Sat.)
  Tuesday (Tues.)

- **You can abbreviate months of the year when you take notes.**
  January (Jan.)   April (Apr.)   October (Oct.)
  February (Feb.)   August (Aug.)   November (Nov.)
  March (Mar.)   September (Sept.)   December (Dec.)
  (May, June, and July do not have abbreviated forms.)

- **You can abbreviate directions when you take notes.**
  North (N)   East (E)   South (S)   West (W)

An *initial* is the first letter of a name. An initial is written as a capital letter and a period. Sometimes initials are used for the names of countries or cities.

Michael Paul Sanders (M.P. Sanders)   United States of America (U.S.A.)
Washington, District of Columbia (Washington, D.C.)

Section 3 Titles

- **Underline titles of books, newspapers, TV series, movies, and magazines.**
  <u>Island of the Blue Dolphins</u>   <u>Miami Herald</u>   <u>I Love Lucy</u>
  Note: These titles are put in italics when using a word processor.

- **Use quotation marks around articles in magazines, short stories, chapters in books, songs, and poems.**
  "This Land Is Your Land"   "The Gift"   "Eletelephony"

- **Capitalize the first, last, and most important words. Articles, prepositions, and conjunctions are usually not capitalized. Be sure to capitalize all verbs, including forms of the verb** *be (am, is, are, was, were, been).*
  A Knight in the Attic   *My Brother Sam Is Dead*

Section 4 Quotation Marks

- Put quotation marks (" ") around the titles of articles, magazines, short stories, book chapters, songs, and poems.
  My favorite short story is "Revenge of the Reptiles."

- Put quotation marks around a *direct quotation,* or a speaker's exact words.
  "Did you see that alligator?" Max asked.

- Do not put quotation marks around an *indirect quotation,* a person's words retold by another speaker. An indirect quotation is often signalled by *whether* or *that.*
  Mark asked whether Rory had seen an alligator.

Writing a Conversation

- Put quotation marks around the speaker's words. Begin a direct quotation with a capital letter. Use a comma to separate the quotation from the rest of the sentence.
  Rory said, "There are no alligators in this area."

- When a direct quotation comes at the end of a sentence, put the end mark inside the last quotation mark.
  Max cried, "Look out!"

- When writing a conversation, begin a new paragraph with each change of speaker.
  Max panted, "I swear I saw a huge, scaly tail and a flat snout in the water!"
  "Relax," Rory said. "I told you there are no alligators around here."

Section 5 Spelling

Use these tips if you are not sure how to spell a word you want to write:

- Say the word aloud, and break it into syllables. Try spelling each syllable. Put the syllables together to spell the whole word.

- Write the word. Make sure there is a vowel in every syllable. If the word looks wrong to you, try spelling it other ways.

- Think of a related word. Parts of related words are often spelled the same.
  Decide is related to *decision.*

Correct spelling helps readers understand what you write. Use a dictionary to check the spellings of any words you are not sure about.

Section 6 End Marks

Every sentence must end with a period, an exclamation point, or a question mark.

- Use a *period* at the end of a statement (declarative sentence) or a command (imperative sentence).
  Dad and I look alike. (*declarative*)   Step back very slowly. (*imperative*)

- Use an *exclamation point* at the end of a firm command (imperative sentence) or at the end of a sentence that shows great feeling or excitement (exclamatory sentence).
  Get away from the cliff! (*imperative*)   What an incredible sight! (*exclamatory*)

- Use a *question mark* at the end of an asking sentence (interrogative sentence).
  How many miles is it to Tucson? (*interrogative*)

Section 7 Apostrophes

An apostrophe (') is used to form the possessive of a noun or to join words in a contraction.

- **Possessives show ownership. To make a singular noun possessive, add *'s*.**
  The bike belongs to Carmen. It is Carmen's bike.
  The truck belongs to Mr. Ross. It is Mr. Ross's truck.

- **To form a possessive from a plural noun that ends in *s*, add only an apostrophe.**
  Those books belong to my sisters. They are my sisters' books.

- **Some plural nouns do not end in *s*. To form possessives with these nouns, add *'s*.**
  The children left their boots here. The children's boots are wet.

- **Use an apostrophe to replace the dropped letters in a contraction.**
  couldn't (could n<u>ot</u>)   it's (it <u>is</u>)   hasn't (has n<u>ot</u>)

Section 8 Commas, Semicolons, and Colons

Commas in Sentences

- **Use a comma after an introductory word in a sentence.**
  Yes, I'd love to go to the movies.   Actually, we had a great time.

- **Use a comma to separate items in a series. A series is a list of three or more items. Put the last comma before *and* or *or*. A comma is not needed to separate two items.**
  Shall we eat cheese, bread, or fruit?   Let's eat cheese and fruit.

- **Use a comma to separate a noun of direct address from the rest of a sentence.**
  Akila, will you please stand up?   We would like you to sing, Akila.

- **Use a comma to separate a direct quotation from the rest of a sentence.**
  Joe asked, "How long must I sit here?"   "You must sit there for one hour," Vic said.

- **Use a comma with the conjunction *and, or,* or *but* when combining independent clauses in a compound sentence.**
  Lisa liked the reptiles best, but Lyle preferred the amphibians.

Semicolons and Colons in Sentences

- **You may use a semicolon or a colon in place of a comma and a conjunction when combining independent clauses. A colon can be used when the second clause states a direct result of the first.**
  Lisa likes reptiles; Lyle prefers amphibians.   Lisa likes reptiles: she has two pet snakes.

Commas and Colons in Letters

- **Use a comma after the greeting and closing of a friendly letter.**
  Dear Reginald,   Your friend, Deke

- **Use a colon after the greeting of a business letter. Use a comma after the closing.**
  Dear Ms. Brocklehurst: Sincerely,

Commas with Dates and Place Names

- **Use a comma to separate the day from the date and the date from the year.**
  We clinched the pennant on Saturday, September 8, 1996.

- **Use a comma to separate the name of a city or town from the name of a state.**
  I visited Memphis, Tennessee.

Sentence Structure and Parts of Speech

Section 9 The Sentence

A *sentence* is a group of words that tells a complete thought. A sentence has two parts: a *subject* and a *predicate*.

- The subject tells *whom* or *what*.   <u>The swimmers</u> race.
- The predicate tells *what happened.*   The judges <u>watch carefully</u>.

There are four kinds of sentences: *declarative, interrogative, imperative,* and *exclamatory.*

- A *declarative sentence* makes a statement and ends with a period.
  Jake swam faster than anyone.
- An *interrogative sentence* asks a question and ends with a question mark.
  Did Sammy qualify for the finals?
- An *imperative sentence* gives a command and usually ends with a period; but a firm command can end with an exclamation point.
  Keep your eyes on the finish line.   Watch out for that bee!
- An *exclamatory sentence* ends with an exclamation point.   Jake has won the race!

Section 10 Subjects

The *subject* of a sentence tells whom or what the sentence is about.

- A sentence can have one subject.   <u>Mary</u> wrote a book.
- A sentence can have a *compound subject,* two or more subjects that share the same predicate.   <u>Alex and Mark</u> have already read the book.
- Imperative sentences have an unnamed *understood subject* of *you* (the person being spoken to).   Give me the book, please. (*Understood subject=you*)

The *complete subject* includes all the words that name and tell about the subject.
     <u>Many students</u> have borrowed the book.

The *simple subject* is the most important noun or pronoun in the complete subject.
     Many <u>students</u> have borrowed the book.   <u>They</u> discussed the book yesterday.
Note: Sometimes the simple subject and the complete subject are the same.
<u>Ricardo</u> is writing a book about robots.

Section 11 Predicates

The *predicate* of a sentence tells what happened.
The *complete predicate* includes a verb and all the words that tell what happened.

- A complete predicate can tell what the subject of the sentence did. This kind of predicate includes an action verb.   Mary <u>won an award</u>.
- A complete predicate can also tell more about the subject. This kind of predicate includes a linking verb.   Mary <u>is a talented writer</u>.
- A *predicate noun* follows a linking verb and renames the subject.
  Mary is a <u>writer</u>.
- A *predicate adjective* follows a linking verb and describes the subject.
  Mary is <u>talented</u>.

A *compound predicate* is two or more predicates that share the same subject. Compound predicates are often joined by the conjunction *and* or *or*.

Ramon **sang and danced** in the play.   Mary **wrote the play and directed it**.

The *simple predicate* is the most important word or words in the complete predicate. The simple predicate is always a verb.

Mary **won** an award for her performance.   She **will receive** a trophy next week.

Section 12 Simple, Compound, and Complex Sentences

A *simple sentence* tells one complete thought.

Arthur has a rock collection.

A *compound sentence* is made up of two simple sentences joined by a comma and a conjunction (*and, or, but*). The two simple sentences in a compound sentence can also be joined by a semicolon. Two simple sentences can go together to make one compound sentence if the ideas in the simple sentences are related.

Arthur has a rock collection**, and** Mary collects shells.
Arthur collects rocks**;** Mary collects shells.

A *complex sentence* is made up of one *independent clause* (or simple sentence) and at least one dependent clause. A *dependent clause* is a group of words that has a subject and a predicate, but cannot stand on its own.

Dependent Clause: when Arthur visited Arizona
Independent Clause: He learned a lot about desert plants.
Complex Sentence: When Arthur visited Arizona, he learned a lot about desert plants.

Section 13 Fragments, Run-ons, and Comma Splices

A fragment can be called an *incomplete sentence* because it does not tell a complete thought.

Sumi and Ali. (*missing a predicate that tells what happened*)
Went hiking in the woods. (*missing a subject that tells who*)

A *run-on sentence* is two complete sentences that are run together. To fix a run-on sentence, use a comma and a conjunction (*and, or, but*) to join the two sentences. (You may also join the sentences with a semicolon.)

Incorrect: Sumi went hiking Ali went swimming.
Correct: Sumi went hiking**, but** Ali went swimming.

A *comma splice* is two complete sentences that have a comma between them but are missing a conjunction (*and, or, but*). To fix a comma splice, add *and, or,* or *but* after the comma.

Incorrect: Sumi went hiking yesterday, Ali went swimming.
Correct: Sumi went hiking yesterday, **and** Ali went swimming.

A *ramble-on sentence* is correct grammatically but contains extra words and phrases that don't add to its meaning.

Incorrect: Hiking through the wilderness to enjoy nature is my favorite outdoor sports activity, probably because it is so enjoyable and such good exercise, and because I enjoy observing wild animals in the wilderness in their natural environment.

Correct: Hiking through the wilderness to enjoy nature is my favorite outdoor sports activity. I enjoy observing wild animals in their natural environment.

Try not to string too many short sentences together when you write. Instead, combine sentences and take out unnecessary information.

> **Incorrect:** I stared at him and he stared at me and I told him to go away and he wouldn't so then I called my big sister.
>
> **Correct:** We stared at each other. I asked him to go away, but he wouldn't. Then I called my big sister.

Section 14 Nouns

A *common noun* names any person, place, thing, or idea.

> Ira visited an auto **museum** with his **friends**. Ira has always had an **interest** in cars.

A *proper noun* names a certain person, place, thing, or idea. Proper nouns begin with a capital letter.

> **Ira** wants to visit the **Sonoran Desert** in **Mexico**.

Section 15 Adjectives

An *adjective* is a word that tells more about a noun or a pronoun.

- **Some adjectives tell what kind.**
  Jim observed the **huge** elephant. The **enormous** beast towered above him.

- **Some adjectives tell how many.**
  The elephant was **twelve** feet tall. It weighed **several** tons.

- **Sometimes an adjective follows the noun it describes.**
  Jim was **careful** not to anger the elephant. He was **happy** when the trainer led it away.

- *A, an,* and *the* are special kinds of adjectives called *articles.* Use *a* and *an* to refer to any person, place, thing, or idea. Use *the* to refer to a specific person, place, thing, or idea. Use *a* before a singular noun that begins with a consonant sound. Use *an* before a singular noun that begins with a vowel sound.
  An elephant is heavier than **a** rhino. **The** elephant in this picture is six weeks old.

- *Demonstrative* adjectives tell which one. The words *this, that, these,* and *those* can be used as demonstrative adjectives. Use *this* and *these* to talk about things that are nearby. Use *that* and *those* to talk about things that are far away.

  This book is about rhinos.   **These** rhinos just came to the zoo.
  That rhino is enormous!   **Those** funny-looking creatures are wildebeests.
  Note: Never use *here* or *there* after the adjectives *this, that, these,* and *those.*

- **A *proper adjective* is made from a proper noun. Capitalize proper adjectives.**
  Italian cooking   **Democratic** convention   **Apache** legend

Section 16 Pronouns

A *pronoun* can replace a noun naming a person, place, thing, or idea. Personal pronouns include *I, me, you, we, us, he, she, it, they,* and *them.*

- A *subject pronoun* takes the place of the subject of a sentence. Subject pronouns are said to be in the *subjective case.* Subject pronouns include *I, he, she, we,* and *they.*
  Incorrect: Rita is an excellent soccer player. **Rita she** made the team.
  Correct: Rita plays goalie. **She** never lets the other team score.

- An *object pronoun* replaces a noun that is the object of a verb or preposition. Object pronouns are said to be in the *objective case*. Object pronouns include *me, him, her, us,* and *them*. The pronouns *it* and *you* can be either subjects or objects.
Rita's team played the Bobcats. Rita's team beat <u>them</u>.
<u>It</u> was a close game. (*subject pronoun*)   The Bobcats almost won <u>it</u>. (*object pronoun*)

- Use a subject pronoun as part of a compound subject. Use an object pronoun as part of a compound object. To test whether a pronoun is correct, say the sentence <u>without</u> the other part of a compound subject or object.
Incorrect: Rita told Ellen and <u>I</u> it was a close game. (Rita told <u>I</u> it was a close game.)
Correct: Rita told Ellen and <u>me</u> it was a close game. (Rita told <u>me</u> it was a close game.)

- An *antecedent* is the word or phrase a pronoun refers to. The antecedent always includes a noun.
<u>The Bobcats</u> are excellent players. (They) won every game last season.

- A pronoun must match its antecedent. An antecedent and pronoun agree when they have the same *number* (singular or plural) and *gender* (male or female).
<u>Nick's mother</u> cheered. <u>She</u> was very excited.

- Possessive pronouns show ownership. The words *my, your, his, her, its, their,* and *our* are possessive pronouns.
Those skates belong to <u>my</u> brother. Those are <u>his</u> kneepads, too.

- A *compound personal pronoun* contains the word *self* or *selves*. Compound personal pronouns include *myself, herself, himself, itself, yourself, ourselves,* and *themselves*. They often show that the action of a sentence is reflecting back to the subject.
My brother bought <u>himself</u> a new puck.   We cheered for <u>ourselves</u>.

- *Indefinite pronouns* refer to persons or things that are not identified as individuals. These pronouns include *all, anybody, both, anything, few, most, no one,* and *somebody*.
<u>Somebody</u> lost the ball.   We can't play <u>anything</u> until we find it.

- The interrogative pronouns *who, whom, whose, what,* and *which* are used to ask questions.
<u>Who</u> has brought the volleyball?   <u>What</u> is a wicket used for?
<u>Which</u> net is used for volleyball?   To <u>whom</u> did you hit the ball?

- *This, that, these,* and *those* can be used as demonstrative pronouns. Use *this* and *these* to talk about one or more things that are nearby. Use *that* and *those* to talk about one or more things that are far away.
<u>This</u> is a soft rug.   <u>These</u> are sweeter than those over there.
<u>That</u> is where I sat yesterday.   <u>Those</u> are new chairs.

Section 17 Verbs

An *action verb* shows action in a sentence.

Scientists <u>study</u> the natural world.   They <u>learn</u> how the laws of nature work.

- A *main verb* is the most important verb in a sentence. An *auxiliary verb,* or *helping verb,* comes before the main verb to help it show action. Auxiliary verbs such as *had, are,* and *will* indicate the tense of the main verb. Others, such as *could, might,* and *may,* show how likely it is that something will happen.
Scientists <u>are</u> studying glaciers.   The studies <u>may</u> help us learn more about Earth.

- The *present tense* is used to show that something happens regularly or is true now. Squirrels <u>bury</u> nuts each fall.

  Add *s* to most verbs to show present tense when the subject is *he, she, it,* or a singular noun. Add *es* to verbs ending in *s, ch, sh, x,* or *z.* Do not add *s* or *es* if the subject is a plural noun or if the subject is *I, you, we,* or *they.*

add *s*	add *es*	change *y* to *i*
speak/speaks	reach/reaches	carry/carries

- The *past tense* shows past action. Add *-ed* to most verbs to form the past tense. Verbs that do not add *-ed* are called *irregular verbs.*

- The *future tense* shows future action. Use the verb *will* to form the future tense.
  Mom <u>will visit</u> Antarctica next year. She <u>will photograph</u> penguins.

- The *present perfect tense* shows action that began in the past and may still be happening. To form the present perfect tense, add the helping verb *has* or *have* to the past participle of a verb.
  Mom <u>has studied</u> Antarctica for years. Her articles <u>have appeared</u> in science journals.

- The *past perfect tense* shows action that was completed by a certain time in the past. To form the past perfect tense, add the verb *had* to the past participle of a verb.
  Before she visited Antarctica, Mom <u>had imagined</u> it as a wasteland.

- The *progressive tenses* show continuing action. To form the *present progressive* tense, add *am, is,* or *are* to the *present participle* of a verb (usually the present form + *-ing*). To form the *past progressive* tense, add *was* or *were* to the present participle. To form the *future progressive* tense, add *will be* to the present participle.
  Scientists <u>are learning</u> new facts about Antarctica every day. (*present progressive tense*)
  When Mom <u>was traveling</u> in Antarctica, she saw its beauty. (*past progressive tense*)
  Someday soon I <u>will be visiting</u> Antarctica with Mom. (*future progressive tense*)

- The subject and its verb must agree in number. Be sure that the verb agrees with its subject and not with the object of a preposition that comes before the verb.
  An Antarctic explorer needs special equipment.
  (*singular subject:* **An Antarctic explorer;** *verb + s or es:* **needs**)
  Explorers in Antarctica carry climbing tools and survival gear.
  (*plural subject:* **Explorers;** *verb without s or es:* **carry**)

A *compound subject* and its verb must agree. Compound subjects joined by *and* are plural. If a compound subject is joined by *or,* the verb must agree with the last item in the subject.

Snow and ice <u>make</u> exploration difficult.
Either the helpers or the leader <u>checks</u> the weather report.

- A verb is in *active voice* if its subject performs an action. A verb is in *passive voice* if its subject is acted upon by something else.
  Explorers <u>plan</u> trips months in advance. (*active voice*)
  Trips <u>are planned</u> months in advance by explorers. (*passive voice*)

A *linking verb* does not show action. It connects the subject of a sentence to a word or words in the predicate that tell about the subject. Linking verbs include *am, is, are, was,* and *were. Seem, appear,* and *become* can be used as linking verbs, too.

Explorers <u>are</u> brave. That route <u>seems</u> very long and dangerous.

Section 18 Adverbs

An *adverb* describes a verb or an adjective. Adverbs tell how, when, where, or how much.

- Many adverbs end in *-ly*. Some adverbs do not end in *-ly*. These include *now, then, very, too,* and *fast*.
  Andrew approached the snake cage <u>slowly</u>. He knew that snakes can move <u>fast</u>.

Section 19 Prepositions

A *preposition* shows a relationship between a word in a sentence and a noun or pronoun that follows the preposition. Prepositions tell when, where, what kind, how, or how much.

- Prepositions include the words *in, at, under, over, on, through, to, across, around, beside, during, off,* and *before*.
  Jeff left the milk <u>on</u> the table.   He knew it belonged <u>in</u> the refrigerator.
- A *prepositional phrase* is a group of words that begins with a preposition and ends with its object. The object of a preposition is a noun or a pronoun. A prepositional phrase can be at the beginning, middle, or end of a sentence.
  Jeff's mom would be home <u>in five minutes</u>. <u>Within three minutes</u> he had put it away.

Section 20 Direct Objects and Indirect Objects

A *direct object* is the noun or pronoun that receives the action of the verb. Direct objects follow action verbs. To find the direct object, say the verb then "Whom?" or "What?" A *compound direct object* occurs when more than one noun receives the action of the verb.

Jacques painted a <u>picture.</u> (Painted whom or what? Picture. *Picture* is the direct object.)
He used a <u>brush</u> and oil <u>paints</u>. (*Brush* and *paints* is the compound direct object.)

A sentence with a direct object may also have an *indirect object*. An indirect object is a noun or pronoun and usually tells to whom something is given, told, or taught.

Jacques gave his <u>mom</u> the painting.

Section 21 Conjunctions

The words *and, or,* and *but* are *coordinating conjunctions*.

- Coordinating conjunctions may be used to join words within a sentence.
  My favorite reptiles are snakes <u>and</u> lizards.   Najim doesn't like snakes <u>or</u> lizards.
- A comma and a coordinating conjunction can be used to join two or more simple sentences. (The conjunction *and* does not need a comma if both sentences are short.)
  I like snakes, <u>but</u> he says they're creepy.   We can get a snake, <u>or</u> we can get a lizard.

A *subordinating conjunction* relates one clause to another. Dependent clauses begin with a subordinating conjunction. Subordinating conjunctions include *because, so, if,* and *before*.

<u>Before</u> his mom left, Bo cleaned his room. He had a favor to ask, <u>so</u> he vacuumed, too.

Section 22 Interjections

An *interjection* expresses emotion and is not part of any independent or dependent clause.
<u>Wow</u>, this bread is delicious!

Section 23 Appositives

An *appositive* is a phrase that identifies a noun.
My favorite snack, <u>cornbread with honey</u>, is easy to make.

Usage

A *negative word* says "no" or "not."

- Often negatives are in the form of contractions.
  Do **not** enter that room.   **Don't** even go near the door.

- In most sentences it is not correct to use two negatives.

  Incorrect | Correct

  We **can't** see **nothing**. | We **can't** see anything.
  We **haven't** got **no** solution. | We **haven't** got a solution.

- The *comparative form* of an adjective or adverb compares two people, places, or things. The comparative form is often followed by "than." To compare two people, places, or things, add *-er* to short adjectives and adverbs.
  An elephant is **tall**. A **giraffe** is **taller** than an **elephant**. (*Giraffe* is compared with *elephant.*)
  A lion runs **fast**. A **cheetah** runs **faster** than **any other animal**. (*Cheetah* is compared with *any other animal.*)

- The *superlative form* of an adjective or adverb compares three or more people, places, or things. The article "the" usually comes before the superlative form. To compare three or more items, add *-est* to short adjectives and adverbs.
  The giraffe is the **tallest** land animal.
  The cheetah is the **fastest** animal alive.

- When comparing two or more persons, places, or things using the ending *-er* or *-est*, never use the word *more.*

  Incorrect | Correct

  She is **more faster** than he is. | She is **faster** than he is.

- The word *more* is used with longer adjectives to compare two persons, places, or things. Use the word *most* to compare three or more persons, places, or things.
  Mario is **excited** about the field trip.
  Duane is **more excited** than Mario.
  Kiki is the **most excited** student of all.

- Sometimes the words *good* and *bad* are used to compare. These words change forms in comparisons.

  Mario is a **good** athlete. | The basketball court is in **bad** shape.
  Kiki is a **better** athlete. | The tennis court is in **worse** shape than the basketball court.
  Bill is the **best** athlete of all. | The ice rink is in the **worst** shape of all.

  Note: Use *better* or *worse* to compare two things. Use *best* or *worst* to compare three or more things.

Section 26 Contractions

When two or more words are combined to form one word, one or more letters are dropped and replaced by an apostrophe. These words are called *contractions*.

- In the contraction below, an apostrophe takes the place of the letters *wi*.
  he will = he'll

- Here are some other common contractions.

cannot/can't	have not/haven't	she would/she'd
could not/couldn't	I will/I'll	they have/they've
does not/doesn't	it is/it's	we are/we're

Section 27 Plural Nouns

- A *singular noun* names one person, place, thing, or idea.

girl	pond	arrow	freedom

- A *plural noun* names more than one person, place, thing, or idea. To make most singular nouns plural, add *s*.

girl<u>s</u>	pond<u>s</u>	arro<u>ws</u>	freedom<u>s</u>

- For nouns ending in *sh, ch, x,* or *z,* add *es* to make the word plural.

bush/bush<u>es</u>	box/bo<u>xes</u>
lunch/lunch<u>es</u>	quiz/qui<u>zzes</u>

- For nouns ending in a consonant and *y,* change the *y* to *i* and add *es*.

penny/penn<u>ies</u>	army/arm<u>ies</u>

- For nouns that end in *f* or *fe,* replace *f* or *fe* with *ves* to make the noun plural.

shelf/shel<u>ves</u>	wife/wi<u>ves</u>

- Some words change spelling when the plural is formed.

man/men	woman/women	mouse/mice	goose/geese

- Some words have the same singular and plural form.

deer	sheep	rice

Section 28 Possessives

A *possessive* shows ownership.

- To make a singular noun possessive, add an apostrophe and *s*.
  John<u>'s</u> bat   the girl<u>'s</u> bike

- When a singular noun ends in *s,* add an apostrophe and *s*.
  Ross<u>'s</u> project   James<u>'s</u> glasses

- To make a plural noun that ends in *s* possessive, add an apostrophe.
  the soldiers<u>'</u> songs   the girls<u>'</u> bikes

- When a plural noun does not end in *s,* add an apostrophe and *s* to show possession.
  the men<u>'s</u> ideas   the children<u>'s</u> shoes

Section 29 Problem Words

These words are often misused in writing.

sit	*Sit* means "rest or stay in one place." Sit down and relax for a while.
sat	*Sat* is the past tense of *sit*. I sat in that chair yesterday.
set	*Set* is a verb meaning "put." Set the chair here.
may	*May* is used to ask permission or to express a possibility. May I have another hot dog? I may borrow that book someday.
can	*Can* shows that someone is able to do something. I can easily eat three hot dogs.
learn	*Learn* means "to get knowledge." Who will help you learn Spanish?
teach	*Teach* means "to give knowledge." Never use *learn* in place of *teach*. **Incorrect:** My sister will learn me to speak Spanish. **Correct:** My sister will teach me to speak Spanish.
is	Use *is* to tell about one person, place, or thing. Alabama is warm during the summer.
are	Use *are* to tell about more than one person, place, or thing. Also use *are* with the word *you*. Seattle and San Francisco are cool during the summer. You are welcome to visit me anytime.
doesn't	The contraction *doesn't* is used with the singular pronouns *he*, *she*, and *it*. He doesn't like sauerkraut. It doesn't agree with him.
don't	The contraction *don't* is used with the plural pronouns *we* and *they*. *Don't* is also used with *I* and *you*. They don't like swiss cheese. I don't care for it, either.
I	Use the pronoun *I* as the subject of a sentence. When using *I* or *me* with another noun or pronoun, always name yourself last. I am going to basketball camp. Renée and I will ride together.
me	Use the pronoun *me* after action verbs. Renée will call me this evening. Also use *me* after a preposition, such as *to*, *at*, and *with*. Pass the ball to me. Come to the game with Renée and me.
good	*Good* is an adjective.
well	*Well* is an adverb. These words are often used incorrectly. **Incorrect:** Renée plays good. **Correct:** Renée is a good basketball player. She plays well.
raise	*Raise* must be followed by a direct object. I raised the flag at camp last summer.
rise	*Rise* does not need a direct object. I had to rise at dawn every morning.

like	*Like* means "similar to" or "have a fondness for." Do not use *is like* to mean "says." **Incorrect:** I enjoy, like, all kinds of water sports. He was like, "Swimming is fun." **Correct:** I like swimming and water polo. He said, "I like the water."
go	*Go* means "move from place to place." Don't use *go* or *went* to mean "says" or "said." **Incorrect:** She went, "The swim meet was yesterday." **Correct:** She said, "I went to the swim meet."
you know	Only use the phrase *you know* when it helps a sentence make sense. Try not to use it in places where it does not belong. **Incorrect:** We can, you know, go canoeing. **Correct:** Did you know that my family has a canoe?

let	*Let* is a verb that means "allow." Please let me go to the mall with you.
leave	*Leave* is a verb that means "go away from" or "let stay." We will leave at noon. Leave your sweater here.

was	*Was* is a past-tense form of *be*. Use *was* to tell about one person or thing. Hana was sad yesterday.
were	*Were* is also a past-tense form of *be*. Use *were* to tell about more than one person or thing. Also use the word *were* with *you*. Hana and her friend were both unhappy. Were you home yesterday?

has	Use *has* to tell about one person or thing. Rory has a stamp collection.
have	Use *have* to tell about more than one. Also use *have* with the pronoun *I*. David and Lin have a rock collection. I have a bottle cap collection.

who	*Who* is in the subjective case and should be used as the subject of a clause. Use *who* to refer to people. The man who picked me up is my father.
whom	*Whom* is in the objective case and should be used as a direct or indirect object or as the object of a preposition. Use *whom* to refer to people. To whom am I speaking?
which	Use *which* to refer to things. His rear tire, which was flat, had to be repaired.
that	*That* can refer to people or things. Use *that* instead of *which* to begin a clause that is necessary to the meaning of the sentence. The picture that Stephon drew won first prize.

very	*Very* is an adverb. It means "extremely." I was very tired after the hike.
real	*Real* is an adjective. It means "actual." Never use *real* in place of *very*. **Incorrect:** The hike was real long. **Correct:** I used a real compass to find my way.

Section 30 Homophones

Homophones sound alike but have different spellings and meanings.

are	*Are* is a form of the verb *be*.	We are best friends.
our	*Our* is a possessive pronoun.	Our favorite color is green.
hour	An *hour* is sixty minutes.	Meet me in an hour.

its	*Its* is a possessive pronoun.	The horse shook its shaggy head.
it's	*It's* is a contraction of the words *it is*.	It's a beautiful day for a ride.

there	*There* is an adverb meaning "in that place." It can also be used as an introductory word.
	Please put the books there. There are three books on the table.
their	*Their* is a possessive pronoun. It shows something belongs to more than one person or thing.
	Their tickets are in my pocket.
they're	*They're* is a contraction made from the words *they are*.
	They're waiting for me inside.

two	*Two* is a number. Apples and pears are two fruits I like.
to	*To* can be a preposition meaning "toward." *To* can also be used with a verb to form an infinitive.
	I brought the pot to the stove. (*preposition*) I like to cook. (*infinitive*)
too	*Too* means "also." I'd like some lunch, too.
	Too can mean "more than enough." That's too much pepper!

your	*Your* is a possessive pronoun.
	Where are your socks?
you're	*You're* is a contraction made from the words *you are*.
	You're coming with us, aren't you?

whose	*Whose* is a possessive pronoun. It can refer to people or things.
	Whose raincoat is this? The raincoat whose buttons are blue is mine.
who's	*Who's* is a contraction made from the words *who* and *is* or *who* and *has*.
	Who's at the front door? Who's got the correct time?

principal	A *principal* is a person with authority.
	The principal made the rule.
principle	A *principle* is a general rule or code of behavior.
	He lived with a strong principle of honesty.

waist	The *waist* is the middle part of the body.
	She wore a belt around her waist.
waste	To *waste* something is to use it in a careless way.
	She would never waste something she could recycle.

aloud	*Aloud* means out loud or able to be heard.	He read the poem aloud.
allowed	*Allowed* is a form of the verb *allow*.	We were not allowed to swim after dark.

Writing a Letter

Section 31 Friendly Letters

A *friendly letter* is an informal letter written to a friend or a family member.

In a friendly letter, you might send a message, invite someone to a party, or thank someone for a gift. A friendly letter has five parts.

- The *heading* gives your address and the date.
- The *greeting* includes the name of the person you are writing to. It begins with a capital letter and ends with a comma.
- The *body* of the letter gives your message.
- The *closing* is a friendly or polite way to say good-bye. It ends with a comma.
- The *signature* is your name.

> 35 Rand Street
> Chicago, Illinois 60606
> July 15, 1997
>
> Dear Kim,
>
>   Hi from the big city. I'm spending the summer learning to skateboard. My brother Raj is teaching me. He's a pro.
>
>   I have one skateboard and hope to buy another one soon. If I can do that, we can practice together when you come to visit.
>
>   Your friend,
>   *Art*

Section 32 Business Letters

A *business letter* is a formal letter.

You would write a business letter to a company, an employer, a newspaper, or any person you do not know well. A business letter looks a lot like a friendly letter, but a business letter includes the name and address of the business you are writing to. The *greeting* of a business letter begins with a capital letter and ends with a colon.

> 35 Rand Street
> Chicago, Illinois 60606
> July 15, 1997
>
> Swenson Skateboard Company
> 10026 Portage Road
> Lansing, Michigan 48091
>
> Dear Sir or Madam:
>
>   Please send me your latest skateboard catalog. I am particularly interested in your newest models, the K-7 series. Thank you.
>
>   Sincerely yours,
>   *Arthur Quinn*
>   Arthur Quinn

Section 33 Addressing Letters

The envelope below shows how to address a letter. A friendly letter and a business letter are addressed the same way.

> Arthur Quinn
> 35 Rand St.
> Chicago, IL 60606
>
>   Kim Lee
>   1555 Montague Blvd.
>   Memphis, TN 38106

Guidelines for Listening and Speaking

Section 34 Listening

These steps will help you be a good listener:

- **Listen carefully** when others are speaking.
- **Keep in mind your reason for listening.** Are you listening to learn about a topic? To be entertained? To get directions? Decide what you should get out of the listening experience.
- **Look directly at the speaker.** Doing this will help you concentrate on what he or she has to say.
- **Do not interrupt** the speaker or talk to others while the speaker is talking.
- **Ask questions** when the speaker is finished talking if there is anything you did not understand.

Section 35 Speaking

Being a good speaker takes practice. These guidelines can help you become an effective speaker:

Giving Oral Reports

- **Be prepared.** Know exactly what it is that you are going to talk about and how long you will speak. Have your notes in front of you.
- **Speak slowly** and **clearly.** Speak **loudly** enough so everyone can hear you.
- **Look** at your audience.

Taking Part in Discussions

- **Listen** to what others have to say.
- **Disagree politely.** Let others in the group know you respect their point of view.
- **Try not to interrupt** others. Everyone should have a chance to speak.

Topic Index

G.U.M.

Language Index